REMEMBER GREENWICH

by

Iris Bryce

This book is dedicated to Betty, my first and dearest friend

ACKNOWLEDGEMENTS

I would like to thank most sincerely the following people without whose help this book would never have been completed:

JULIAN WATSON and his staff at Greenwich Local History Library
ROGER NORMAN Editor South East London & Kentish Mercury Group
MRS BEAGLES Halstow Road School
KATH BISHOP for patiently typing out my first manuscript
REBECCA my daughter for the beautiful presentation of the final draft
and most of all to the late HARRY DAVIS,
Borough librarian of Greenwich, who gave me so much encouragement in those early days.

GREENWICH
COMMUNITY
COLLEGE
PRESS

First published in Great Britain by
Greenwich Community College Press 1995
Corelli Road London SE3 8EP. Tel: (0181) 319 8088.
Printed by The Granby Press Ltd London.

ISBN 1 874678 10 3

Photographs supplied by:
Halstow Road School
Greenwich Local History Library
Iris Bryce

Some of the names in this book have been changed for personal reasons.

GREENWICH
COMMUNITY
COLLEGE
PRESS

INTRODUCTION

The Greenwich Community College Press has been set up with the intention of providing a platform for local writers on local issues. As its second publication, the Press is publishing Iris Bryce's remarkable evocation of a working-class childhood in Greenwich during the 1920s and 1930s.

The Press is particularly privileged to be in a position of introducing Iris Bryce's recollections of childhood to a wider audience because the book was the joint overall winner of the National Life Story Awards 1994 (as well as joint winner of the written category). The awards are administered by the National Life Story Collection at the British Library National Sound Archive. The aim of the awards is to encourage people to put on record their experiences and the story of their lives.

'Remember Greenwich' is a finely observed and deeply expressed portrait of Iris Bryce's childhood in Greenwich. The account brings alive in a very powerful and poignant way characteristics of working-class culture against the backcloth of Greenwich's familiar landmarks and past history.

I have no doubt that the book will appeal to a wide audience, both within Greenwich and beyond. It is just the kind of locally rooted and colourful account of community life which the Press is keen to support!

Dr Terry Powley
Principal Greenwich Community College

January 1995

FOREWORD

When I read the manuscript of this book I was deeply impressed not only by the illuminating content but by the quality of its writing. It was one of a large number of manuscripts submitted for the first national oral history competition in this country organised by the British Library National Life Story Awards, and in an extraordinarily strong field it was an outstanding joint winner.

The book speaks for itself. Iris Bryce has had distinctive experiences of her own which she chronicles beautifully. She also has the rarer gift, however, of describing common experience in a highly distinctive way. Her book is a valuable contribution both to literature and to social history. It deserves to be widely read.

ASA BRIGGS
January 1995

Further information about the British Library National Life Story Awards can be obtained from:
National Life Story Collection
29 Exhibition Road
London SW7 2AS

CHAPTER ONE

I hated those cobbles, whether being bumped over them in my push-chair, learning to ride a bicycle, or teetering in my first high-heeled shoes... it was always the cobbled part of our street that let me down, and not only physically. I felt they degraded the street - and me.

My push-chair, a home-made effort of which I was its fourth occupant, consisted of a fabric seat and back supported by wooden frames. I have clear memories of being pushed up and down the street, although I have no recollection of who was pushing... although it must have been my sister. She was twelve years older than I and in the tradition of our street I was one of her daily chores. I never really knew her as she was always that mysterious being, a grown-up. In later years we had so little in common that our paths rarely met.

But as far as our street was concerned, the world into which I was born in the middle of the twenties was little changed from that of the previous generations. There were certainly no celebrations at my birth as I timed it to be followed by newspaper headlines of the General Strike. The family already consisted of Mum, Dad, sister Daisy and brother Fred (another sister had died aged four, two years before I made my appearance). Dad was a skilled tradesman, a barge-builder, but he had returned from World War I only to join the ranks again - this time of the unemployed, until being taken back by his old firm. After I was born Mum went out to work full-time and it was Gran and the street who took care of me.

My education began in that tight community which kept so much to itself, the same families living and dying in the little bricked terraced houses generation after generation, where baby's cot was squeezed in the corner of the parents' room until Gran and Grandad died when the extra space was immediately seized by the expanding young family.

Each of the smoke-stained, dusty streets and alleys of Greenwich kept strictly to itself. Even the children formed into gangs that fought regularly to prevent children from foreign streets coming to play in theirs. And our street felt this isolation even more because we were a higgledy-piggledy assortment of buildings and alleys that led nowhere; a cul-de-sac of bizarre shape.

First, the street was really two streets, both cul-de-sacs. Woodland Street ran from the main Woolwich - Deptford road with a pub standing on one corner and a grocer's on the other. Facing our street on the opposite side of the road stood a church with a vast square tower and four pinnacles overshadowing us half the day. The lower part of the street was cobbled with huge black and dark grey, rounded shiny stones, and the tiny pavements, skirting each side, were surfaced with decorated herringbone paving bricks. Where the cobbles ended the street divided into an alley on the right, with the backs of the main road shops opening on to it. At the end of the alley another street, Woodland Grove, ran off to the left. The gardens of the houses on the left-hand side of the Grove ran back to back with the gardens of the houses on the right-hand side of the street.

Twelve houses stood on each side with one large cream-coloured plaster-faced house standing alone at the top. By the side of this house was another tiny alley with another three houses facing the opposite way to the large house, their gardens running back along the alley, meeting the side of the twelfth house on the left-hand side of the street.

The cream house was one of mystery and it and its occupants were different. For one thing it was of an unusual design, much larger than any of the other houses, with almost twice as many rooms. But what set it apart was the fact that it was divided into lodging rooms which were looked down upon by the rest of the neighbourhood. Not that any of us owned our own houses, but we didn't share our front doors with any but family, except out of necessity if an elderly person had been left alone, when it was considered respectable to take in a lodger - who was usually given the front parlour and back bedroom. The old house at the top of the street had an ever changing stream of lodgers who stayed a week or so and then disappeared. We neither knew who they were nor what they did, and as children were forbidden to speak to them. They were not of the street. The one exception was the old witch who had a room downstairs, at the front. She, we knew, was a witch. Her wispy white hair hung about her shoulders and she wore several skirts at a time and hugged beautifully crocheted shawls around her thin shoulders. On cold or windy days, in the fashion of old women at that time, she wore a man's peaked cap. In summer she would perch on her windowsill, smoking a small pipe, filled usually with dried tea-leaves, or sit in a rocking chair on the pavement and we would stand and watch, from a safe distance, as her flying fingers crocheted yet another lovely shawl.

We lived at Number twenty, which was the second to last house at the top of the street. From my bedroom window I could look down on her, standing in the sooty night and I'd hear her call, "Nigger, Nigger, Nigger"... it was always in threes, until her cat appeared, to sidle against her skirts, when she would turn and float into the darkness of her passage, the animal following.

But the rest of that household merely shadow my childhood memories; they put down no roots in our solid, unchanging background, and I realise now how much they missed. When I moved away I knew deep down that my roots were still there, a feeling intensified whenever I return to my native Greenwich.

CHAPTER TWO

At no time as a child can I remember loving or feeling loved for, family life then was almost non-existent. Mum, Dad, sister and brother each led a separate existence and I, who was eight years younger than Fred, the next youngest was made to feel the odd one out. Obviously unexpected, certainly unplanned I was sometimes looked at with surprise when I spoke as if they could not believe I was really there. So for comfort I turned to the street and its people, their comings and goings, above all to the children and characters like Arthur, the coal merchant's youngest son, whom I met when I was four years old and remained a friend of his for the next eight or nine years.

Three sons lived with their widowed mother in the Grove and ran a coal delivery round. Their horses and carts were stabled in the alley between the Street and the Grove. Arthur, the youngest son, was of medium height with broad shoulders and muscular arms. He was less bright than his brothers but the children loved Arthur as he was on our level. The older children called him doo-lally-tap, meaning he was mentally retarded, and the adults smiled as they passed him as if he were a favourite pet. But I came to know Arthur well and would watch him muck out the stables or sack coal knowing he was happiest when he was with his beloved horses.

Every evening I would wait for the carts to return and as soon as I heard the clip-clop of their hooves on the cobbles I would race to the stables. Here Arthur's coal-begrimed face would dissolve into white creases, his smile widening while he carefully backed the horse and cart through the gateway into the microscopic yard. He would lead the horse from the shafts, remove the reins and bits and, once stabled, he would lovingly brush them down, throw an old blanket over them and give them their feed.

This nightly routine I saw hundreds of times, but only from the top of the coal yard gate as I was terrified of horses ! I thought Arthur the bravest man in the world to go so near to those wicked-looking hooves (until I discovered the blacksmith in Fenton Street and saw how he handled them.)

Next to the coal yard was a jumble of corrugated and wooden sheds which was the wheelwrights, another small family business run by a father and his three sons. Their father lived in the Grove next door to my Gran, and a son lived next door to us. A second son also lived in the Grove while the third son lived two or three streets away, and since he was virtually a foreigner I hardly knew him at all.

Children could always be found outside the wheelwright's yard watching the fitting of heated metal rims over the outside of wooden wheels. We heard the hiss as wheel and rim came into contact with the water vat beneath the wheel and the swearing as father and son struggled to fit the rim exactly as father wanted, "this bloody way boy, to me, to me. There, you cowson, that's got you". By now the sweat would be running off their faces, shirts stuck to their backs. If it didn't go right first time the old man would turn on us, shouting "clear off you bloody lot, how's a man to bloody get on with you grinning bastards always under his arse". But we knew him so well that we never went - so long as we touched nothing in the yard or got in his way we knew that come November Fifth he would arrange one of the largest bonfires in the town. And we could scrounge as much sawdust as we wanted from him to fill the legs and arms of Dad's old clothes to make our guy. There would be potatoes cooked in the ashes and jugs of cocoa and of course fireworks. Some children would have their own but the bulk were provided by the wheelwright, this night was his spectacular treat.

All too soon it was over, but not before buckets of water had doused the bonfire, the ashes raked again and again to ensure no smouldering embers remained, since adjoining were a ramshackle collection of wooden sheds and huts which would have gone up in flames in minutes had we been careless.

Arthur's beloved horses were tethered on a waste piece of ground at the top of the Grove on bonfire night and not until the last banger had exploded and the final rocket fired into the sky would Arthur, a bridle in each hand, return them to the stable, murmuring softly to calm his faithful friends.

Our Gran luckily lived on the side of the Grove whose gardens backed on to ours for it saved our legs when we wanted to tell her something as we could just shout across the back fences. There was one drawback, well two really; first her garden didn't quite meet ours as she was about three gardens down, and secondly she was a little deaf. But if after several shouts of "Gran, Gran" had failed to bring her out then Aunt Elsie who lived next door to her would call over her fence or bang on her kitchen wall and then Gran would emerge. Aunt Elsie was not a real aunt; all grown ups who were particular friends of Mum and Dad had to be called Aunt and Uncle for some reason. Several such lived nearby and although Mum and Dad both came from large families I seldom met my genuine aunts and uncles.

I can remember being puzzled during school lessons when I learned about relationships in families, but my street aunts and uncles were always more real to me than those of my own blood and more important, they were always there. Aunt Dora was my favourite; she was also my godmother and had been present at my birth. I was born at four minutes to midnight on February 21st according to the midwife but Aunt Dora, whose own birthday happened to be on February 22nd, insisted that it was after midnight and my birthday was the same as hers. The midwife was adamant so my birth certificate says February 21st to Aunt Dora's disgust.

I spent much of my school days with her and for three years she gave me my midday dinner. I can recall now the appetising smells that greeted me from her basement kitchen. She was a marvellous cook who followed a strict routine so that we ate the same meal on the same day every week. To this day I think of Tuesdays as stew... Wednesday, liver and bacon and Thursday is still shepherds pie.

Aunt Dora's was the only house in the street to boast a basement. It was called the area, 'airy' to the children, its window protected by an iron grille across the pavement. The gap between the grille and the window was just large enough to allow a ball to roll through and most days you could find a group of children crowding and calling for the return of their ball. A favourite ball game entailed bouncing the ball with one hand and swinging one leg over it between bounces, singing at the same time "one, two three a-lairy, my ball is down the airy, how many times is that?" and according to how often you bounced the ball without failing to swing a leg over it, the winner was declared.

In the kitchen by the area window sat Grandfather Nightingale, in his high-backed wooden armchair. He was Dora's father, a sailor who had travelled the world "round and round like a bleedin' top" he would say. Now retired he sat all day in the kitchen, reading his paper and talking to Poll, his parrot which he had brought ashore from his last ship. Even though Aunt Dora disliked it she had to put up with Poll in her kitchen. I loved the bird and it was Poll and Grandfather Nightingale who taught me to say my first words; they also taught me a lot of other words that caused Grandfather to laugh and made Mum and Aunt Dora cross. Grandfather Nightingale said the parrot liked me so much that I could have her when he died. Poll was a great talker and loved to show off. When we sat down to dinner she'd say "gis a bit, gis a bit" and Grandfather would put a piece of meat on to his fork and, leaning back, would push it through the bars of her cage. She refused to say "thank you" or even "ta" no matter how hard I tried to teach her. She would grasp the meat in her curved beak and return to her perch where holding it in one claw, she would tear it into strips and eat. If there were visitors Grandfather would show her off... after a few "gis a bits" he would offer the meat, but this time dipped in mustard. On tasting this Poll would throw the meat against the bars of the cage shouting "sod you, sod you, sod you". Aunt Dora would redden with embarrassment while Grandfather would chuckle away; after wiping his eyes he would murmur and coo and reward Poll with a piece of chocolate. She could sing and whistle but if children crowded round the area window, making it too dark for Grandfather to read, the moment he shook his fists at them she would shout "clear yer bloody 'ook".

At night Poll's cage was covered with a length of black velvet behind which you could hear her softly humming as she settled to sleep. But if anyone was playing the piano, or we had a party, she would scream abuse until we uncovered the cage and let her join in. When Grandfather died I took over ownership but after so many years Aunt Dora decided she could not bear to part with her. I saw and fed her daily, cleaned her cage, and always of course chatted to her. She knew my step on the basement stairs and would greet me as I came in through the doorway, "hallo old girl". When I grew up and left home it was a wrench

5

leaving her behind. Within six months Mum wrote to say she was dead. At the end, Aunt Dora said, she wouldn't eat and her eyes had developed a milky film. The vet could find no disease and not knowing her age found it impossible to say what had caused her death. He did say however that parrots had been known to pine for people they liked. As she had lost Grandfather after twenty years and then me after another fourteen perhaps she simply missed her two best friends and cleared her hook.

CHAPTER THREE

The houses opposite had railings projecting about two feet on to the pavement for what purpose I don't know as it certainly wasn't to enclose any gardens for there was no soil to be seen - just asphalt. Where perhaps one or two railings were missing the horizontal bar across the top became an athletics bar and we would curl our legs over it and hang upside down, crawling with our hands on the ground and emerge on to the other side of the railings. A forfeit for losing marks in a game, or breaking a rule, was to walk along the top of the railings, feet between the spikes, with a penalty of starting again from the beginning if you fell off. Usually all the damage we did to ourselves was torn knickers or trousers and a scratch or two. No-one was ever spiked.

For the more courageous the arm of a lamp-post offered a challenge. For the less adventurous it was sufficient to throw a rope over the arm and make a swing. But to show off we would climb the lamp-post and use the arm as a trapeze. Here we dangled by legs or arms, and would swing and turn over and over until with a deep breath we would let go and fall to the ground.

The top half of the street contained some smooth patches in the asphalt on which we chalked out hop-scotch games; throughout the whole of my time in the street there was always one somewhere in the middle of the road. Of course there were crazes for other games that would be played by all for months on end, until suddenly no-one played them and they would soon be forgotten as we would go on to yet another craze. Hop-scotch however remained a perennial.

Most of our games had been handed down to us by elder children and they had changed very little over several generations, but in the thirties we were introduced to new games, mostly from America. In the event of the game needing special equipment it would be some time before the street adopted it, having to wait for someone to have a birthday or perhaps a Christmas present consisting of the latest gimmick. Po-go sticks were one, but they never took on in our street, the cobbles put a stop to that... yo-yo's soon were cheap enough to be sold in Woolworths and most of us had one in our blazer pocket ready to take out and challenge anyone to see how long we could continuously manipulate it up and down the string without getting it knotted or losing its momentum. Some children became very competent with yo-yo's and performed all kinds of tricks with them; they competed at the local cinema for fantastic prizes and how I envied the lucky winner who took home a brand new bicycle!

A new bike was almost unheard of among us; we usually had our brother's or sister's hand-me-down or, as in my case, we hired them. I learned to ride a bike by saving up my precious halfpennies earned by running errands, and hiring a bike from a woman who lived in a similar street to ours near the riverside.

7

She had about half a dozen very old bikes for which she charged a penny an hour. All along the street, outside her house you could see children wobbling along on these decrepit machines until that almost magic moment when you found that you were actually going along in a straight line, and you realized that you COULD RIDE A BIKE!

But it was in the street that we played our favourite games, games like five stones. Any summer evening you would find a gang of us sitting on the kerb, and you would hear the click as the stones were thrown into the air, to be caught on the hand, and then if you were expert you started picking them up from the ground, one at a time, throwing a master pebble into the air and catching it, and picking up from the ground at the same time... and all the time a soft chanting from the player as he or she progressed through the several stages of the game, 'into the air' ... 'turn the mangle' ... 'through the door' ... we all had our own sets of five stones; like lucky charms, you polished and cherished them and found it really difficult to let anyone else use your specials.

There were also many team games. Tin-Can Copper was one we played a lot, and very often a grown-up brother returning from work would join us. We all loved the game, but our parents didn't. It was set up much like cricket; someone batted with a piece of wood and we used a tin instead of a ball. The tin was thrown, the batsman would give it a swipe and as it rolled down the street the bowling side would start kicking it further and further down. The batting side had to try and hide. When the tin had been recovered by the batsman the search would start for the rest of his team - a Hide and Seek, in fact, but each time a member was found they had to kick the tin back up the street. When everyone was discovered another batsman went in. When all had had a go at the bat the sides changed. This game took a long time to play and usually before it was finished an irate parent would demand the tin with a voice that brooked no argument.

So we would then play something quieter, like Statues, or We Come to Town to Get Some Work. This latter entailed miming the kind of work we wanted with a leader guessing the occupations.

We put on lots of concerts, dressing up in old curtains and bedspreads and parading up and down the street, crooning the latest songs and performing somersaults, cartwheels or walking on our hands.

The rusty iron wheel rims lying around the wheelwright's yard made good hoops to bowl along, although these went better on the main road where the pavements were smoother than on our wretched cobbles. The shoppers, however, would swear as we brushed past them whacking our hoops with bits of old iron. Whips and tops were cheap to buy and as they took up little room we played with them on the top part of the street. Some tops were the wooden kind with colours painted on which merged into patterns as you whipped faster and faster, but we also had peg tops. These were conical shaped pieces of wood which had a metal pin in the bottom. String was wound around and around the top and you pulled this quickly, unwinding the top which set it spinning on the metal pin - if you were expert, that is. I always had trouble with mine, but Mum proved adept at this and when she could be persuaded to leave her housework for a moment or two she would start mine off for me on our smooth doorstep.

The one thing I longed for when I was about eight years of age was a pair of roller skates ... it seemed as if everyone had a pair of skates except me. I stood for hours outside Nobles, the toy shop in Trafalgar Road, looking at the really super skates they sold for ten shillings ... an unheard of amount for a child to possess. The nearest I ever came to that was when Dad's brother, Uncle Joe, popped into see us on his days off from work. He was a lighterman and worked shifts, sometimes 24 hours on and 48 hours off, most of the latter spent in the pub. From time to time he would come to our house to sober up before facing Aunt Ada, and it was on these occasions that he usually gave me sixpence; once he even threw me half-a-crown. But no matter how much I gazed at the skates I knew that nothing short of a miracle would make them mine. I had already asked for them for my birthday and for Christmas too, but instead had come the usual new clothes and books which, although welcome, were overshadowed by my desire for the skates - then my miracle happened. Our Fred won a prize on the football pools. I think it was £70; anyway he gave Mum, Dad and Daisy some of it and with a pat on the head he handed me a ten shilling note ! How I ran down the street, along Trafalgar Road and straight into Nobles's. I had the pair out of the window, and the box they put them in became as much as a treasure as the skates themselves.

After each skating session they were religiously wrapped up in the tissue paper and replaced in the box, the very first thing that I had ever bought myself. They were my very own, and I never got over the thrill of feeling I was flying as I skated down the street - that was until I came to the cobbles. I soon learned to jump on to the pavement when I reached them but the patterned bricks there were not much better. Once on the main road, the large paved slabs were lovely and smooth and my wheels just glided over them, jumping off the curb and on up the other side, weaving in and out of the shoppers. Of course they didn't like us skaters any more than they did the hoop-bowlers, and they would shout and swear after us, but in a flash we were up and away out of reach of threatening fists and walking sticks.

Later I even used them to go to school in Halstow Road which was over a mile from home, but complaints from people who lived nearby soon had the Headmistress giving us a good talking to, and that was the end of skating to and from school.

It was not very often that we invited each other into our houses to play. If we had been ill and were still confined to the house then one or two of us would be allowed in to play Snakes and Ladders, Ludo, or Fishing, but Mum did not like me going into other houses and she never encouraged other children into ours. She was averse to what she called the gossips in the street, who forever seemed to be running in and out of each other's houses, usually on a pretence of borrowing a bit of tea, or some condensed milk, but staying to have a chat which seemed to be endless.

Mum and Dad, having lived in the street since they were married before World War I, were accepted and had their own set of friends but we knew, and the rest knew, that somehow Mum did not fit in with the other women, and some of that offence was passed on to us children. At first I did not realise this but by the time I started school I knew that I didn't fit completely into the pattern of life which surrounded me, the life led by our neighbours, my playmates and the street itself.

CHAPTER FOUR

It was just after my fourth birthday when my world collapsed. Life up to then had been Mum giving me food when I was hungry, her skirts for me to tug on and learn to stand and walk, and once on my feet I'd been put into the street every morning to play with the other toddlers.

And then came the morning when I awoke to find no Mum and no breakfast on the kitchen table, just Daisy who dressed me and then to my astonishment bundled me into my outdoor clothes. My cries for "Mum", my questions and finally my tears went unnoticed by Daisy who just pushed me about, doing up gaiters, tying a big scarf around my chest and pinning it at the back. Then grabbing my hand, we set off down the street, round the corner and along to the Grove where, with a push on my backside, Daisy bade me, "run on up to Gran's and bang on the door". I stood sobbing, looking at her in bewilderment, only to receive another push in the back, "Don't be daft, go on", and through my tears I saw her walk back down the Grove where she waved, calling out "ta-ta" as she disappeared round the corner. I stood sniffing and sobbing and then realising I was alone I ran and ran until I reached Gran's. I kicked and banged on her door. I could hear her grumbling long before she reached it. "Shut up that banging, shut up". Then the door opened and there she stood, dressed in her clean white pinny, over her long grey skirt and two or three petticoats, her streaky grey hair done in a knot at the back of her head. Her arms were bare to her elbows, her sleeves were always rolled up once she got indoors. "Can't work with stuff messing around your hands", she'd say.

I followed her into her kitchen and the sobs gradually died away as she unpinned my scarf and expertly unhooked my gaiters, leaving me to remove my coat, beret and gloves.

Gran's house was built much the same as ours, but her stairs went in a spiral from her kitchen, whereas ours went straight up from the side of our passage, and Gran's were a soft white wood, ours were covered in dark lino. Her kitchen always seemed neater and tidier than ours, although Mum being her daughter our house was always clean and tidy too. Gran's kitchen table was scrubbed white like the stairs and her scullery always had a lovely smell of cooking about it.

It seemed to me that whenever I visited Gran she had a rabbit soaking in a white enamel bowl. Rabbits were bought whole from the butcher with their skin still on and it took Gran, a country-bred girl, no time at all with a sharp knife to slit up the skin from the belly. The two hind legs were pulled through first, then the skin was pulled straight up the back, the two fore-legs pulled out and last of all the head. Finally the slippery pink and grey body would be immersed in cold water "to draw the blood, make him nice and white". Today the smell of rabbit stew takes me straight back to Gran's scullery. She was also famous for her apple dumplings and made them for many a young housewife who was 'heavy with pastry', including Mum who had not inherited Gran's skill. Although Mum was a good plain cook I can remember her making few tarts, cakes or pies, but then Mum's life did not leave much time for frills.

Gran was born in Bures, a tiny village in Suffolk, deep in the heart of Constable country, the third daughter of farm labourer Daniel Cardy and his wife Elizabeth. Life was hard in rural England during the middle of the nineteenth century and Gran had taken on her share of farm-work at an early age, having to pick peas or potatoes before breakfast. If she overslept then her father woke her with his leather belt. Her mother, my great-grandmother, was built up to be a romantic figure. Gran told us that she was really Lady Elizabeth Cresswell who had fallen in love with her coachman, Daniel Cardy, with whom she eloped and married. Her father had immediately severed all connections and cut her out of his will. Gran told many stories of her life as a child and her mother figured always as a gentle, loving creature, far above the mean hard life she led for the rest of her days.

I loved to hear Gran tell me these stories but this morning she did not seem inclined to talk; she just mumbled to herself as she sat me down on one of the big wooden armchairs that stood on both sides of the shiny black-leaded fireplace. I sank back into one of her big soft patchwork cushions.

"What's all this crying then?"

"W-w-where's me Mum?"

"It's not right, she should 'ave told yer 'erself. She's got a job, down at the rope works, so you're to have some breakfast with me every morning afore you go to school".

The word 'school' meant nothing to me. No-one had talked to me of school, no-one in our house went to school; they all went to work, that is except me Mum. No, the word that did mean something, the one that made my tears disappear immediately was 'breakfast' and soon I was watching Gran cut up my 'soldiers' to dip into the yolk of a soft boiled egg. Mrs Coleman, who lived next door to Gran, kept chickens in her backyard and Gran was supplied with fresh eggs, like most of the other families in the Grove. I loved a boiled egg but Gran would put on a lot of salt which I hated but I daren't leave any of my egg. I did once and it was served up cold the next morning ... so salty as it was I learned to eat all my egg every morning plus my soldiers and a cup of strong sweet tea, sweetened with condensed milk.

Packets of cereals were fairly new to our street but Mum sometimes bought Force or Shredded Wheat. However as we had fresh milk delivered about twice a week we seldom had them for breakfast. Sometimes we ate Shredded Wheat spread with butter but breakfast at home mainly amounted to a cup of tea and a slice of bread and jam during the week. No-one bothered about a balanced diet; we ate a lot of bread, and had meat about twice a week, always a joint on Sunday of course.

12

With the exception of rolled oats for porridge Gran considered packets of cereals to be rubbish and so for the next year or so I breakfasted on boiled egg, or porridge, or sometimes on cold winter mornings a bowl of hot sweet cornflour, once again sweetened with condensed milk.

That first morning, after I had finished my breakfast, Gran went upstairs to see to Grandad and I followed her up the spiral staircase to the tiny front bedroom where Grandad lay in bed. He had had an accident at the Gasworks where he had been a labourer and ever since then he had just lain in bed. He hardly spoke, but understood everything Gran said to him. To me Grandad looked like a great big cuddly bear; he had thick snow-white hair and must have been quite a big man, for although his body was sunk deep into Gran's home-made feather mattress he still made a hugh mound beneath the white honeycomb quilt, which was also home-made. I wished I could have known him better; he looked so kind and gentle, and Gran said he was the finest man to walk God's earth.

 He too came from Suffolk, a farm labourer who had met and married Gran. As two young newly-weds they had come to London to find their fortune towards the end of the 1870s but all they found was poverty and near tragedy. Grandad had worked only with animals on the farm and he could not adjust to the industrial skills that this factory orientated area of South East London demanded. His first job was looking after horses - those that pulled the horse buses - and he worked on the route between New Cross Gate and Blackwall Lane. But as these gradually went out of fashion he lost his job. With an ever-growing family there were many days when starvation faced them. Gran cleaned and scrubbed and as the girls grew big enough to carry a pail of water they too were soon out scrubbing doorsteps before going to school. But the money coming in was never enough to feed the family properly and when Gran discovered escape via the cheap gin-shops standing on most corners, things became desperate.

Grandad eventually succumbed to stealing. He went into a baker's near Westcombe Hill and stole a loaf ... of course he was such an amateur that he was caught immediately. Gran never said if he went to prison; she always said, "he had his punishment". However, the story went around Greenwich and about two months later Grandad was offered a job as general labourer at the Gasworks. Then shortly afterwards he fell down a flight of steep metal stairs on the outside of a building, and that was the end of Grandad as an active man. He died when I was six years of age and to me his death meant missing those lovely warm times when I sat by his bed and he held my hand and smiled at me with his eyes while I told him new nursery rhymes or made up stories for him. But on this day I stood inside the door and heard Gran tell him that she was just going to take me to school, get a bit of shopping and be back to make him some Bovril. He nodded and smiled at me, and we went down the steep winding stairs, to get dressed in all my outdoor things again.

CHAPTER FIVE

I held Gran's hand as we walked along Trafalgar Road past Fenton Street, where I saw the blacksmith shoeing a horse and we turned up the next street then crossed over a road. Never before had I been so far from home; hitherto the street had been my boundary. We passed some large grey-bricked buildings standing behind tall railings, went through a gate in the railings and crossed a yard to one of the smaller buildings.

Gran opened a big glass door and we climbed a flight of stone steps facing us. Up we went, round and round, up and up and at last Gran knocked on a door painted such a dark brown that it had become one with the dark brown walls of the stairs. A clear bright voice called out "Come in", Gran opened the door and in we went. The first thing I remember is the smell which came from a saucepan standing on a griddle over a coal fire in a tiny fireplace. Inside the saucepan was something dark brown and bubbling, and I immediately fell in love with that romantic, bitter smell.

It was some four or five years later, after I had been made a monitor and helped in the staff room, that I found out what that smell was ... coffee made with freshly ground beans, or berries as Miss Tilly called them. Miss Tilly could not really have been as old as Gran but she looked just the same to me. Her grey hair ran tightly in little waves across her head; she was very thin, and wore unusual spectacles in thin silver rims, only the bottom halves filled with glass.

While she and Gran talked I looked at the room which was small and crammed with chairs and two large desks. One wall was covered with bookshelves. This was the Staff Room and there were books, magazines, papers, pencils, pens, cups and saucers, every surface was cluttered. Miss Tilly rose from her desk and bent down in front of me. "Well, are you ready to come with me and meet your new friends? Say goodbye to Grandma. She'll meet you at the gate at dinnertime". I willingly gave her my hand for I liked her, and I liked this place too. There was so much to look at, to touch, to do. Downstairs we passed through another door on the ground floor and I was handed over to Mrs Norton.

I was told to sit at a desk in the front row next to another little girl who, like Miss Tilly, wore glasses, only hers were large and round. I had not met any children wearing glasses before and I found myself staring at her with delight. I took to my new life like a duck to water; what a lot of things to do, people to play with, toys, sand in trays and my favourite, books, lots of them. I was glad to be at school, with one exception; 'milk and malt' at playtime.

Before we went out to play we had to queue up in the hall where we were given a spoonful of malt and a mug of milk. This was handed out by a vast old lady called Mrs Waters who lived in a dirty old house at the top of the next street to ours, and she smelt. I didn't know then of course but a combination of unwashed clothes, unclean body and general lack of hygiene caused this odour. Her hands were grey with dirt ground into them and the milk she ladled out into enamel mugs was a bluey colour. I felt sick as soon as I started to drink but I soon learned to sidle slowly to the door outside which a drain stood conveniently placed for me to pour away the milk.

The malt I could not avoid as Mrs Waters stood behind a huge tin equipped with two spoons; one in your mouth and the other straight back into the tin for the next child. I complained nightly about this to Mum, but no-one ever listened to me. As a family we went our own way and if I did keep up a constant moan I either received a slap or was just told to "shut up, it's for your own good". Milk and malt apart, I loved school. I found learning to read perfectly natural and once I had mastered it I was seldom found without a book in my hand. My world had opened like an oyster. I read and read and read.

By the time I was five I had been going to Gran's for breakfast on my own for some time. Daisy had been glad to get rid of the job as it gave her more time to put on her face each morning. Most days my feet found their own way to the Grove as my nose was deep in a book, looking at new pictures, mouthing new words. Gran made me have breakfast sharp at seven which was the time Arthur would be getting the horses ready so I soon started hanging about the stables watching him and his charges. Arthur couldn't read and he always wanted to know what my current story was about, so over the years we read together The Water Babies, Black Beauty, The Little Prince and later on the William stories which he loved. Once the horses and carts had gone out Arthur and I would sit and read some more until it was time for me to go to school. He enjoyed these reading sessions and told me how clever I was. I in turn loved having an audience.

CHAPTER SIX

By the time I was six it was decided that I could get my own breakfast and not bother Gran; so it was back once more to tea and bread and jam. I was also old enough now to take on a share of the housework. Everyone had at least one special job to do in the house; once a week Daisy scrubbed the passage from the front door through to the scullery; Fred had to clean and sharpen the cutlery, all except the carving knife which only Dad was allowed to touch.

And now my job - virtually a daily chore - was to lay the fire and light it when I got home from school; I also had to have the kettle boiling in time for Mum when she got home from work, and later have the table ready laid for tea.

We always had a large pot of tea and something hot like beans on toast, sausage and mash or my favourite bubble and squeak, which was a fry-up of vegetables left over from a previous meal, using mostly cabbage and potato. And of course always we had bread, butter and jam. Our only proper hot meal was Sunday dinner and Monday night stew.

Monday stew was Dad's cooking night ... he always made a stew every Monday night, using the meat left over from the Sunday joint, which had already been used again for sandwiches to take to work on Monday morning. Dad would fold back the kitchen tablecloth after tea when he had finished washing up (his regular evening household job). He would bring in from the scullery a large enamel saucepan half filled with cold water into which he would carefully slice the remaining meat from the bone using a small sharp pocket knife. Dad was particular about both his large carver and his small pocket knife which were kept razor edged by constant sharpening on our back-door step. When the bone was bare and shiny he would toss that into the saucepan as well and then he would peel and chop up a potato, carrot, turnip, onion and any other potherb available, add salt and pepper and put the saucepan on the gas stove with a small flame underneath. A Foster Clark's tomato soup cube was crumbled and well stirred in. By the time Dad got back from the local, round about ten, the stew was ready.

Each of us was given a large plateful before going to bed; the rest was earmarked for Tuesday tea with maybe the addition of some dumplings if Mum had time when she got home. I stood by Dad's side Monday after Monday watching him chop up vegetables, wondering how he did it so quickly without cutting his fingers. Every now and then he would pop a piece of raw carrot or whatever he was chopping into my mouth and I developed a taste for raw vegetables which has remained throughout life. I still amaze one old friend by my liking of raw potato! "Give you a good clear skin", said Dad and I must admit I never had too much trouble with spots.

No dinners were provided at school so while still in the Infants I went back to Gran's, but once I had entered the Junior side of Maze Hill School I wanted to be like the other children and go to the fish and chip shop or better still, the eel and pie shop, or even buy hot faggots and pease pudding. Mum didn't like the idea at all and said it wasn't nice to walk about the streets eating out of newspapers, well at least not at dinnertime. It was different at night when everyone did it as they left the pub or pictures.

But after a while she relented and once a week, on a Friday, she gave me threepence and I joined some of my school friends at the eel and pie shop at the top of Blackwall Lane. The menu was hot pie and mash with liquor, hot eels and mash, or jellied eels; all for threepence a big plateful. The hot pie and mash was my favourite, because I loved the big spoonful of hot 'liquor' poured liberally over the top of it, a thin grey fluid with pieces of parsley chopped in it, but far removed from any parsley sauce I tasted in later years - to my childhood palate that liquor tasted better than any gravy, be it Mum's or Gran's.

I returned to Greenwich recently and while in a baker's shop near Blackwall Lane I mentioned to the manageress how sad it was to see that the eel and pie shop had gone. She had no idea what I meant and said she had lived in Greenwich for years and there had never been one standing opposite her shop. Well I can assure her there was in the twenties and thirties.

If it was pease pudding and faggots for dinner then we got them from the butcher on the corner, opposite the pie shop. I was never really fond of faggots but loved the pease pudding, the best to be had was when Gran and I went to the pictures and took a basin with us and on the way back we stopped to buy some for supper.

Saturdays were curious days for me. The mornings were filled by running errands for anyone in the street, or just hanging about the house waiting for Mum to come home from work at twelve o'clock, but as I grew older I was given the job of removing the sheets and pillowcases from the beds ready for Mum to wash when she came in. I had also to light the copper in the scullery and get the water hot.

On her way home Mum would buy the vegetables and joint for the weekend. As soon as she had put these down in the kitchen she would have her coat and hat off, apron on, sleeves rolled up and not stopping for a cup of tea she would start the weekly laundering.

First of all the clothes had to be sorted; white, coloured, Dad's and Fred's working clothes, then underclothes, and socks last of all. Mum and I would stand surrounded by piles of washing in the scullery while the water boiled in the copper; then she would get the oval tin bath off the back yard wall and put it on a trestle in the yard. The water was then ladled out of the copper into an enamel bowl and carried out to the bath. Her scrubbing board hung on the yard wall and with this and a bar of Sunlight soap she started on the weekly wash.

I fetched and carried water, swished the blue-bag in the final rinsing water, and helped turn the wheel on our big iron mangle with its wooden rollers. Dad had provided a really high line-pole and while I held the peg bag Mum proudly hung her washing in the yard to dry. She loved washing and ironing, and she was expert at it. Thanks to her days of service as a chamber-maid at the Trafalgar Hotel we were the best turned out family in the street; she saw to that.

The Trafalgar was once a famous hostelry, dating back to Lord Nelson's days when it was called the George. Over the years this Greenwich pub on the banks of the Thames had been a favourite eating place of politicians, including Mr Gladstone, and the political whitebait suppers became well known affairs. Charles Dickens frequented it and used it as a background to the wedding feast in 'Our Mutual Friend'. But towards the end of the nineteenth century the Trafalgar was turned into a beer house and the rooms used as a sweet factory. However in 1895 a Mr George Damiral was granted a lease of twenty-one years and once again the Trafalgar became a hotel, but not in the grand manner of former times. At the age of fourteen Mum had been put into service to the housekeeper employed by Mr Damiral and there, along with another young slavey, Mum learned how to run a large house. The laundering was Mum's speciality and, although she loved to put her arms elbow deep into bowls of soapy water and scrub away at shirts and sheets, she did not enjoy carrying the heavy baskets of wet clothes up to the roof where they were pegged out to dry. And what a wind she had to contend with, coming straight off the river round the corner from Blackwall Reach!

One night when Mum was going off duty she was summoned by the bell clanging in the downstairs kitchen and on going to the entrance lobby she saw the housekeeper talking to a man and a boy of about seventeen who had just arrived and wanted a room for the night. Mum showed them to a first floor apartment and asked if they wanted supper. The man asked for tea and toast while the boy, who looked ill, remained silent, and Mum later took their order up to them. They left early next morning to catch a boat from Greenwich Pier down the Thames.

A few weeks later Mum was called to the housekeeper's room where she was questioned by two detectives about the man and boy she had served a few weeks previously. She answered as best she could, mentioning how ill the boy looked and remarking that he hadn't spoken at all. It was then she was told that the boy had in fact been a young woman, Ethel Le Neve by name; the man was Dr Crippen, the American-born doctor from Michigan, who had come to England and married an actress, Belle. The marriage was far from happy and soon the doctor fell in love with his secretary. After a party at their home in Holloway, Dr Crippen had killed his wife, disposing of her body in a way that had shocked the world. They had stayed one night at the Trafalgar before crossing to the continent and taking ship to America where they were arrested on arrival thanks to the use of the newly invented and installed radio-telegraph by an astute Captain. Suddenly a young chambermaid found herself in the middle of this horrific story, but for her and the rest of the working class it was just a nine days wonder after which humdrum routine soon took over, almost erasing the incident from memory ... in fact it was some fifty years after the event that Mum ever thought to tell us about it.

And so standing by Mum's side on Saturday afternoons I watched and learned her art of laundering; on Sunday afternoons or evenings I would run to and fro with the two black flat irons which we heated on the stove in the scullery. These were cherished possessions. Mum always used the kitchen table for ironing, placing a blanket over it to give a firm smooth surface. Skilfully she ironed to a satin smoothness the shirts, blouses, and twisting rapidly between the frills and pleats of Daisy's skirts. Even when electric irons were common, after a while Mum went back to her favoured flat irons.

I was allowed to iron the handkerchiefs, Mum watching to see I didn't skimp the borders; each had to be ironed round the borders, then the middle, finally a pressing after each fold.

As the pile grew higher so did my pride but no matter how hard and how long I tried I never became the expert laundress that Mum was. Even today in her eighties, with her flat iron and no ironing board still, just her table, she makes a better job of my husband's shirts than I could ever do. Even Dad's coarse working shirts were as carefully laundered as his Sunday best; nothing slipshod when it came to laundering in our house.

Not until the washing was on the line would Mum sit down for a cup of tea when I would run down to Woolworths for a pound of broken biscuits costing twopence (or threepence if you wanted cream ones included). Saturday dinner would be somewhat late but we would enjoy our cups of sweet tea into which we dunked our biscuits. I always hoped for lots of ginger ones as these were my favourite.

Washing for a family of five was a chore, especially after a week's work in the rope factory, but never once did you hear Mum grumble; in fact almost the reverse. For as soon as Mum started on housework she started to sing.

She had a good voice and told me that a lady had heard her when she was scrubbing steps as a child and had asked her mother if she could go for lessons to have her voice trained but Gran had said there was no time for that kind of thing. But training or not Mum had a voice that made people sit and listen, and she taught me the ballads of World War I, the music hall songs, while I reciprocated with crooners' songs of the thirties.

Although I did not inherit her voice I did her love of music and together on Saturday afternoons we would sing as we poured out water, scrubbed collars and cuffs and swished the blue-bag round, Rose of No

Man's Land, Bye Bye Blackbird, Over my Shoulder goes One Care ... and the mangle turned to Shirley Temple favourites or perhaps a wartime Comrades. This intimacy between Mum and me never went any further; once the washing was done I was returned to the land of childhood ... to be seen and not heard.

CHAPTER SEVEN

None of the family apart from Mum was around much on Saturday afternoons. Dad and sometimes Fred with him would be at a football match if the local team, Charlton Athletic, were playing at home, or Fred might be at the dog track at Charlton or Catford. Daisy seemed to spend the afternoon buying another frock or pair of shoes; she had masses of clothes and was very fussy about her stockings. I can remember the arguments when she threw them away if they had a tiny ladder or hole in them. She simply would not wear stockings with a ladder, not even if Mum repaired them for her so neatly that you could hardly see it.

She bought most of her dresses at Rose's just past Blackwall Lane. They cost about five shillings. Shoes could be bought in Deptford High Street for half-a-crown a pair but you could pay ten shillings if you wanted to be in the fashion.

Of course both Daisy and Fred had to pay Mum something towards the house- keeping but they always seemed to have plenty to spend upon themselves. Sometimes if they were generous I would be given sixpence on a Friday night, but this wasn't very often. Both quietly tucked away money in the Post Office Savings. Daisy, in particular, was very secretive about her money; in fact it seemed to be a subject that no-one talked about much. Mum never discussed how hard up we were, nor did she ever reveal just how much money she had. Throughout Dad's life she never knew just how much money he earned; every week he simply gave her thirty shillings up to the forties when he gave her a rise and made it two pounds a week. With that Mum was supposed to pay the rent, insurances and feed us. No wonder she was always working, worrying and wondering how to deal with the next emergency. Dad never worried. Not once in the whole of his life did he ever give a thought for the morrow ... he enjoyed today.

He was a selfish man, who considered no-one else at all. As I grew up he would urge me to enjoy myself, live for today, and always remember to look after number one first - the latter being of course, yourself. Every night he sat and read the paper before having his few glasses of beer. If he didn't feel like going down to the Crown, then I would be sent down with the jug and he would drink in the kitchen, oblivious to Mum who was working non-stop from teatime until she went to bed. He did however insist on taking her out with him when he went out drinking at the weekends.

The pub on the corner of our street did for casual midweek drinking but Saturday night and Sundays called for dressing up in your best clothes with maybe a walk through Greenwich Park to The Ship in King William Street or perhaps the Admiral Hardy in Greenwich Market.

Once a month on a Sunday morning there was a ritual visit to sister Eileen's grave in Shooters Hill

Cemetery. I would help Dad tidy up the grave for a sister I had never known; Mum always seemed sad on these Sunday mornings and I seemed to be forgotten momentarily as she re-lived the few years she had had with her baby daughter.

The ritual was always followed by a walk across the Nine-Fields which led to a pub called The Fox Under The Hill. Here I could run through wild grassland, climb over fallen tree trunks and watch the officers from the Royal Artillery Barracks ride their horses across the fields, over the road and on to Woolwich Common. I spent many Sunday mornings alone wandering over the Nine-Fields, watching the birds and wondering what they were called, throwing sticks for dogs to chase. When Dad and Mum came out of the pub I would be told off for scuffing my best shoes, or dirtying my Sunday dress.

They wouldn't listen to my chatter about the birds or dogs and it was the same at home, no-one wanted to know about school or how I had seen the horses being shod at Fenton Street forge. Dad would rustle his paper irritatedly; Fred might be studying form as he called it when he started reading about horses and greyhounds; Daisy would be chatting to Mum about the latest Hollywood fashions and I would be told, "for Christ's sake stop nattering". Questions were either ignored or "wait and see - you'll soon find out". Soon I learned to keep things to myself, to sit with a book and keep quiet, and by doing so I often heard things not meant for me. I would pretend that I was invisible, seated on my little wooden stool in the corner of the kitchen, nose in book, head bent. But inside I was lonely and longed for a real friend, for although there were plenty of children to play with in the street and enjoy games with, I felt attached to none in particular. The fact that I went to Maze Hill School was one of the barriers in forming a friendship. For some reason unknown to me, Mum and Dad did not want me to attend the school attached to the church at the bottom of the street. Both Daisy and Fred had gone to Christ Church School, as did most of the children living in the street and it was of course much nearer than Maze Hill School. However I was the odd one out and throughout my early school years walked alone every day.

When I discovered the book on school life written by Angela Brazil I found this wonderful new life became my escape; how I longed to have chums, to go to school in those lovely old houses. I did not know what French grammar was but I felt I'd like to have a chance to find out ... how lucky those girls were. I was puzzled for years about the girls going to the nets after tea. What did they practise at the nets? It was many years later that I discovered they were for cricket and not for fishing and of course all the girls looked so attractive in their school uniform ... I wondered if I would ever wear a gym-slip and white blouse.

There was a school on the other side of Greenwich which did have a similar uniform and I'd seen one or two of their girls waiting for the tram; after reading Angela Brazil I took a new interest in them.

22

CHAPTER EIGHT

Up to the age of nine I accompanied Mum and Dad on their drinking nights at the local pubs. Like many other children I became a leaner against the doors and walls ... every now and then catching a whiff of warm, tobacco-laden air when the doors opened. I wasn't forgotten by my parents and Dad would come out once or twice during the evening with a drink and biscuit. It was always the same, a glass of grapefruit and an arrowroot biscuit, measuring about three inches across, and always very dry and crispy. I usually gave the second one to one of the many dogs lying about the pavement. I envied other children eating potato crisps but Dad said there was no goodness in them; occasionally however I could have a packet of cheese biscuits. About nine-thirty someone would ask Mum to sing and I would sit on the steps of the private bar and hear her singing again the words we had sung at the washtub. Dad sang too, very funny music-hall songs that obviously had two meanings to them.

Both Mum and Dad were favourites at their locals, but they didn't normally drink to excess; there was rarely the money for that. At times of course Dad did get drunk and even Mum might have a little trouble in speaking clearly. They did spend quite a lot of their weekly income in the pubs, but when you consider the life they led, who can really blame them; in fact it was their only escape.

Mum's life was just a round of work either in the rope factory or in the home. She never had a holiday; in fact none of us did. Dad didn't get paid holidays and anyway he always said he couldn't see why people wanted to go away and sleep in a strange bed, eating strange food. He liked Mum's cooking and his own bed and asked for nothing more.

I suddenly realised that I did want something more; I did not like leaning up against pub walls for three hours at a time, and so I asked Mum if it was all right for me to stay at home instead of going out with them. Neither she nor Dad objected so from then on Saturday nights were spent alone in the house.

I saved my weekly Schoolgirl comic from Thursday so that I could savour it in my solitude, and of course I always had a library book, but on the first Saturday night by nine o'clock I found myself wandering up and down the stairs, along the passage to look out of the front door and back again into the kitchen ... what could I do with myself? It wasn't much use going to bed before the pub shut because on Saturday nights the door of the gents banged continually, its padlocked bar whacking the brickwork as each customer came and went.

I heard the boy next door start to play the piano so I sat down in the passage and leaned against the wall to hear better. He played on and on, all the dance tunes, the crooners' songs. He was good and Fred said he played like Charlie Kunz, but as we had neither a gramophone nor a wireless I had not heard Charlie

Kunz; but I did like the music I heard through the wall.

I wished I could play that way since it was so much better than Mum's style and sounded so right. Then I did something rather daring; I went into the front parlour, opened our piano and very softly, with one finger, I started to play. The piano was our most treasured possession, our one gesture to living up to the Jones's. We had one because it was the thing to do, not because anyone played it, properly that is. In fact Mum was the only person up to that time whom I had ever heard play our piano, and now I was actually sitting down and playing it myself. I soon discovered that I could pick out the melodies fairly easily but I quickly became frustrated, not knowing what to do with my left hand. I sounded just like Mum when she plonked her left hand up and down, up and down and apparently no-one but me noticed how discordant it always sounded. How I enjoyed discovering the pleasure of playing the piano, but not to the extent of forgetting the time. It would not do to have Mum and Dad return and find me in the parlour. I was in bed when they came home but far from asleep, trying to think up ways of persuading them to let me have music lessons. I just had to find out how to play the piano properly. I woke early on Sunday morning and immediately remembered my excitement of the night before. I dared not move too much or too quickly as I shared the bed with Daisy who liked a lie-in on Sunday mornings. I got some pretty sharp slaps if I woke her too early.

I lay and looked around the bedroom, at the aspidistra plant in its shiny blue artpot, standing on a tall bamboo pedestal in the window; the net curtains across the bottom half of the window were firm and taut, while the long pink curtains swayed gently at the sides. Our bedroom walls were distempered in pale green and Daisy had covered her side of the room with photos of Ramon Navarro cut out of her film magazines. They were framed in silver paper and looked down on her as she lay in bed.

A dark brown dressing table with three mirrors stood beside the window and this was all Daisy's territory. A glass oblong tray stood in the centre of the dressing table and behind this were pots and tubes of creams and rouge; a large glass powder bowl with a white fluffy powder puff stood beneath the mirror. Underneath another mirror seven small green elephants walked across a black bridge bearing on their trunks Daisy's rings which she had bought in Woolworths. They were silver rings with coloured glass stones, the light from the window reflecting in them and the mirror sending pin points of colour up to the ceiling. There were also scent bottles, lipsticks, brush and combs, a manicure set in tortoise-shell, none of which I was allowed to touch, but which of course I did whenever I got the chance. I was clever though in replacing them and I carefully put back hair slides and bottle tops in their exact positions.

I was terrified of being discovered in some wrong doing as Dad had a terrible temper. When I was very young I saw Fred thrashed many times with Dad's leather belt for some youthful adolescent misdemeanour. Most of the children in the street stole off the stalls; apples, oranges, a carrot to munch, and they took sweets from poor Miss Hussy's shop in Earlswood Street as a matter of course. Although I was often with them and enjoyed sharing their spoils I could never bring myself to actually take anything. I longed to, desperately thinking it would make me really belong to the gang who universally considered me a baby and a coward, but at the back of my mind was always Dad with his leather belt. Suddenly Daisy moaned making me instantly alert; making sure that I kept well away from her body I moved my feet to my side of the bed. As she settled into her pillows again I studied her face from which she religiously cleaned off all her paint and powder at night and replaced with a layer of thick cold cream. In the morning her face would still be shiny with thin streams of white cream clinging to the sides of her nose. One plucked eye-brow showed up blackly against her skin, like half a bracket; her high cheek bones seeming to pierce the surface. As I grew older most of my girl friends told me how attractive my sister was which came as a surprise to me. I knew that Daisy slavishly followed the fashions of the film stars in Hollywood. She plucked out her eyebrows completely and pencilled them back in; her nails were blood red which Dad hated, and she wore floppy dresses with short wide matching sleeves or no sleeves at all. On this particular Sunday morning I could not lie in bed any longer so, slipping quietly out of my side, I dressed quickly and went downstairs. Mum was in the scullery cooking the ritual breakfast of the week; bacon, tomatoes, kidneys and mushrooms for Dad and Fred, bacon and tomatoes for Mum and me; toast and tea for Daisy when she finally rose. If Dad was in a good mood then a piece of kidney would be slipped on to my plate, but best of all was mopping up the tomato gravy with bread. If I finished mine before Dad then I could have his plate to wipe as well.

That Sunday morning started so well that I wondered if I could pluck up the courage to mention the piano lessons. Mum asked what I'd done with myself the night before, which was so unusual that I found myself reddening and mumbling, as I wiped my bread round my plate, that I had read my comics and books. I wondered if Mrs Dalton next door had heard me on the piano and told Mum? I knew this was not the time to ask about piano lessons. Dad just said I would ruin my eyes with all that reading, but once again Mum surprised me by smiling mysteriously and saying she would have to think of some way to help me spend my Saturday nights. Did she really know about the piano?

I could hardly wait for the week to pass and Saturday to come again. When it did Mum came in the kitchen in her best clothes and smilingly gave me two magic painting books, the kind you brush with water and the colours come through the pictures. I took them in silence realising that she meant well.

Once the front door shut behind them I let the hot tears slide down my cheeks; magic painting books and I were light years apart. I had obviously inherited some of Dad's temper for the next moment I was raging

25

about the house, slamming doors, tearing my comics and the wretched painting books; then I sat and wept. Loneliness overcame me; I went to the front door and stood on the step watching the people walking past the street, in and out of the pub, and the trams and buses going along the road. Should I go down and see if my parents were in the Crown? I knew however that I didn't really want to. Full of despair I only knew that all I wanted to do was to escape from the street and the family. Even the piano failed to tempt me, I simply went to bed and prayed that the years would pass quickly and that I would grow up and be able to leave the street and all it stood for. Childish dreams and plans tumbled through my mind but in every one was a growing resentment of the way of life to which I'd been born.

CHAPTER NINE

Once I was in the junior school at Maze Hill the resilience of childhood took over and I found life had much to offer. Lessons seemed easy and apart from constant bad marks for poor writing, and a complete blockage when it came to knitting the standard six inch square iron holders for our mums, I found myself top of the class in most tests. I thought it unfair that I lost a great number of marks in arithmetic because my paper was not neatly presented; however most of the class found great difficulty in 'doing sums' while I still kept near the top in spite of untidy writing.

The school time-table consisted of arithmetic, reading, writing, spelling, geography, history, religious instruction and PE or physical exercises. The first four were given far more time than the rest of the subjects which were sketchily covered throughout the rest of my time in junior school.

PE we came to dread. We were drilled in long straggly lines, either in the playground or the hall clad only in our knickers and vests shivering while Miss Harvey, in a short navy blue serge skirt and cream blouse, instructed us to jump up and down, wave our arms, run on the spot, touch our toes and take deep breaths all without lifting up your shoulders. Poor conscientious Miss Harvey led the exercises herself; as she was extremely short and very fat it wasn't long before those of us lucky enough to be at the back of the class would be grinning and trying to hold in our laughter along with our breaths. But you couldn't fool her for long and our stifled giggles would turn to gulps of terror as she suddenly lunged forward and with a grip of iron dragged one of us to the front of the class there to perform solo. I grew up loathing anything to do with sport, even the rare excursions to Greenwich Park where we raced between avenues of chestnut trees at the top of Observatory Hill.

The teachers at the junior school were strict and used the ruler almost daily on the knuckles of some luckless pupil who had forgotten how to spell or add, or generally misbehaved in the classroom. Teachers seemed to find it necessary to leave us alone at least once a day and strict warnings were always given of what would happen if any unruly behaviour or noise occurred during this absence. Of course as soon as her back was turned someone would throw an ink bomb across the room starting a rumpus which lasted until 'Miss' returned.

The most dreaded punishment was to be sent to the headmaster, Mr Nixon. He was large and stout and his forbidding appearance towered above us - clutching his cane he demanded to know why we had been sent to him. Whatever the reason, whether fair or unfair, great or small, the answer was always the same ... a whacking with the cane. But on the whole I found school days at Maze Hill fairly easy-going and none more so than on Empire Day. This was an important celebration both for the school and town. Red, white and blue ribbons and other streamers together with Union Jacks were put up outside windows and strung across streets, while shop windows were dressed with red, white and blue rosettes. At school we wore white dresses with red, white and blue sashes, and similarly coloured ribbons in our hair, while boys had red, white and blue ties and belts. In the afternoon a lucky chosen few danced around the maypole which was set up in the playground, in front of our parents, friends, the staff and governors of the school. This was followed by the Maze Hill prize-giving ceremony.

To be chosen for the Dance was an honour and an ordeal, for woe betide anyone who turned right instead of left, or in when they should have danced out. If this happened then, instead of our splendid ribbons entwining in beautiful geometric patterns round and down the pole, they degenerated into a nightmare of enmeshed streamers that became more and more knotted as the dancer numb with horror allowed other dancers to go round her, thus adding to the confusion and then when the numbness wore off, the culprit would stare up at the pole and try to work in reverse to free the offending ribbon, thereby making the original disaster more chaotic. But by the morning of May 24th the chosen few would be so well drilled that it was rare for anything but a first rate display. This was nothing short of a miracle when you realise that the teacher responsible was our PE mistress, Miss Harvey.

The maypole was erected at the far end of our asphalt playground with chairs facing it. A small table stood to the side of the pole, well out of the reach of the flying ribbons and feet, on which sat a small wind-up gramophone. Miss Harvey shouted out her instructions, rushed over and wound up the gramophone, placing the needle on the somewhat worn record. The trouble was the playground stood between the railway line and the road leading to Maze Hill station, and although there were few cars using the road, there were plenty of trains, so often her instructions were swallowed up in a loud whistle and cloud of steam as a train emerged from the tunnel underneath Greenwich Park before entering Maze Hill station. Other noises came from the road where the rag and bone man daily trundled his horse and cart, steel rims rattling over the asphalt road and iron bars and old pots banging against each other as he slowly circled the railings crying "any old iron?" But whatever the obstacles on Empire Day, the uniformed dancers waited impatiently for the off, then how we would dance and almost fly around, stopping for a fraction to show off our completed pattern before unwinding until the pole again stood shiny and bare, the victorious ribbons clutched in our sweaty palms.

The audience always clapped and a few bravos would be heard. After a thank-you speech by the headmaster, the prize-winners were called to the dais where the Chairman of the school governors handed out the prizes. Girls invariably seemed to get Mrs Beetons's Cookery Book, one to which I always aspired.

Prizes were only given to pupils in the top class who were leaving for other schools after the summer holidays. When my turn eventually came I was astonished to receive, not the coveted cookery book, but a writing outfit in a snakeskin case. It was a beautiful thing, containing not only paper and envelopes, but pen, pencil, rubber, a tiny wallet for stamps, a notebook, and a box for spare pen nibs.

Was psychology behind this prize? All the teachers knew how badly I wrote; was this beautiful paper and pen to make me produce readable copy in the future, or was it because I had not only won a prize for general school work, but also a scholarship to a famous grammar school? I can remember feeling sad because no-one from the family was present to see me walk up and receive my prize, or ask me what the Headmaster had said when he stopped to talk to me. I missed having no Mum to show my prize off to when I returned to my seat.

GREENWICH
COMMUNITY
COLLEGE
PRESS

Photographs supplied by:
Halstow Road School
Greenwich Local History Library
Iris Bryce

The author is standing at the left end of the front row.
Maze Hill School 1930

Above: Grandad and Gran Hills. Back garden Woodland Grove, 1930
Below: Trinity Hospital, dwarfed by the neighbouring power station

Above: author is third from left, second row from top, Halstow Road School 1937. Miss Bell is the teacher.

Right: Ship Hotel,
now the site of the "Cutty Sark".

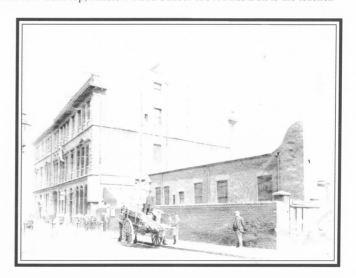

May Day at Halstow Road School, circa 1934

Halstow Road School, 1938

Barnards cinema, bombed in World War II and now the Greenwich Theatre

East Greenwich Library

Aerial view of Siemans Brothers Ltd

Above: Press shop, Siemems
Above right: Cable Yard, Siemens
Right: Greenwich Observatory

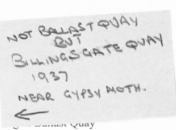

Bottom left: Stockwell Street showing Barnards cinema far right

Bottom: Ballast Quay

CHAPTER TEN

By going out to work all day, Mum was in a minority and I think she was criticised by most of the other women in the street because of it. Only one other woman worked full time and she had no children of school age. Many of the women openly showed their pity for my coming home to an empty house. They really believed a woman's place was in the home and that it was up to the man to provide the money to run it.

Few households survived on what the man alone brought in and most women in fact did work, mainly as charwomen. Many of my school mates woke up to find that Mum had left the house an hour or so earlier and was busy scrubbing out offices, shops, banks and schools. But these children also knew that when they went home for dinner Mum would have something for them, even if it was just bread and jam and a cup of tea.

My mum was different from the others because she rarely swore whereas bloody, fuck, sod and shit were laced liberally in most sentences heard in the street.

Quite a lot of young boys wore their older brothers' cast offs and it was a common sight to see a small boy shuffling along in boots at least two sizes too big and trousers with gaping holes or patched with different material. Jackets would be frayed at the sleeves which were cut to a suitable length and the shirt tails of big brother's old shirts were always showing through the bottom of short trouser legs.

But I was different; Mum saw to that. I was not allowed out with a dress that had a button missing, or holey socks and I daren't go out to play without changing my school shoes for plimsolls. On Sundays I had a best outfit and there was something new for me to wear on Easter Sunday.

Although my clothes were new to me they were in many cases - dresses and coats especially - hand-me-downs. One of the 'aunts' in the street had a sister who had married well and lived in North London in a smart new house. She had a daughter the same age as me and an arrangement was made that Mum would buy all the dresses that Joyce had grown out of or was tired of, as well as any coats because these were expensive to buy new. I looked forward to these arriving and spent time parading up and down in front of the mirror trying on the various garments. But Joyce started growing faster than me and my dresses had to be taken up and taken in, while the coats hung over my shoulders, the sleeves reaching my finger nails. Although I started to look a figure of fun, Mum was adamant that I had to wear them, telling me how lucky I was to have them at all.

She would recall her own childhood as the middle of a large family, a father unemployed, a mother discovering escape in the gin bottle. Mum had been sent out scrubbing doorsteps when she was seven, almost too small to carry her bucket from house to house; and the large lump of white hearthstone had to be broken into suitable lumps for her small hands. Every morning before school she had four doorsteps to clean, and then with the twopence she had earned she would go to Jobbins the baker's in Blackheath and buy yesterday's bread and buns. You could get six buns for a halfpenny, a sum which would also buy a large cottage loaf. If she didn't spend all the twopence then the rest was for her mother's morning gin. This had been the start of Mum's hard life and now her aim was to see that her children would not go hungry or badly shod. She had a dread of weekly expenses outstripping income, and would rather work in the rope factory than rely on Tusons the pawnshop used so regularly by many of the other women. At the front of the queue outside Tusons each Monday morning you would always see an old woman wearing a man's cap and pushing a pram which contained clothing. Old Mr Tuson knew the wardrobes of many men in Greenwich as their suits, overcoats and jackets came in on Monday mornings to pay the rent, and were reclaimed each Friday after wage packets had been opened. But he never got to know Dad's or Fred's, thanks to Mum.

There was a period however when for some reason or other we found ourselves in the hands of a money-lender and it soon fell to my lot to visit him every Friday night to repay by weekly instalments. At first I looked forward to this as the money-lender lived in New Cross - well away from our home town - and I had to take a tram from Trafalgar Road to his office in Amersham Road.

Tram rides were still a novelty to me even though I was nearly ten, as our small world rarely went beyond Blackheath or Charlton, and we always walked to these places. It took us nearly three years to repay what we had borrowed and although I started off enjoying my weekly Friday adventure I soon felt how sordid the whole thing was and the excitement faded. I never did find out why we had needed the money or what had gone wrong with any of Mum's plans.

I began to notice how slovenly and miserable the underground office was in the money-lender's house ... and how furtive and mean-looking the other people were who waited with me in the outer room. I started feeling dirty myself and shrank from going in, imagining that everyone on the tram knew that I was bound for the money-lender and that the other people who got off at the same stop, especially if they walked along Amersham Road as well, were just there to watch me enter the broken gate, walk along the overgrown path and down the four steep steps to the basement.

Once inside I would stand in a corner, not caring to look at the women with their shawls tucked across their breasts, some wearing men's peaked caps, or the men in creased trousers with shrivelled hand-rolled cigarettes sticking to their bottom lips.

The money-lender sat behind his desk in a room which was like an airless cupboard. Behind him a dirty window reflected a wilderness similar to the front garden, but this time at the rear of the house. He always seemed to me to be wearing the same dark suit with a wide chalk stripe, looking up from a ledger only to take the money and enter it before putting the amount, date and his signature on our payment card which I clutched.

I was thankful to escape outside again and usually ran down the road to wait for the next tram. I always enjoyed the ride home, especially as we bumped round the corner at Greenwich Church where the conductor jumped off and ran along the middle of the road to pull a lever and change our course along towards Trafalgar Road - otherwise we would have gone straight on to Creek Road.

Returning home one Friday night I was sitting in the front seat upstairs which was my favourite because from here I could imagine I was driving this red clanging metal monster. The rails sped swiftly beneath me and I rocked back and forth as we gathered speed along Greenwich High Road; then the bell clanged furiously as at the fork of South Street we joined the trams on routes 58 and 62 coming from Lewisham. We passed the almshouses and as Greenwich Church came into view I grabbed the front rail 'helping' the driver to slow down. I saw the conductor had jumped off and was almost at the lever but I couldn't quite see what happened as he pulled it so I decided to leave my seat and run back down the tram to look from the back window. Just then the tram lurched heavily and leaned over to one side. One of the few passengers upstairs started to shout as the tram shuddered again and leaned the other way, then it slowly ground forward and rocked gently to a stop, following a crash of glass. The tram had jumped the points and left the rails and the front seat where I had been sitting was now embedded in the front of a shop in Nelson Street, but still upright and with no-one hurt. A crowd appeared and an ambulance from the Miller Hospital seemed disappointed that there were no casualties; meanwhile the passengers waited for another tram whilst the broken glass was already being swept up.

As I lived only about half a mile away I walked the rest of the way home past the Royal Naval College and the Queen's House. The latter was a boys school and on Sunday mornings they paraded in naval uniform and marched across the main road from the Queen's House into the Royal Naval College for church service.

I liked this part of Greenwich where the buildings were large and gracious. The lawns were like green velvet with wide gravel paths, and in front lay the river with the park behind. I pressed my face to the railings and wondered if I would ever see inside, and walk along the colonnade which links the two wings. Many years afterwards when the National Maritime Museum took over the buildings this did indeed become a well-loved place to visit, but on that particular Friday night I didn't linger, I was filled with the drama, and dying to retell my tale at home.

As I handed over the payment card and answered the usual questions, I waited for Mum to ask why I was so late.

"Did he sign it, has he put the right date on?"

"Yes Mum".

"Did he say anything?"

"No Mum." And there was nothing more ...

" I'm a bit later getting back tonight, did you notice?" No reply, she had gone into the scullery to carry on with whatever housework I had interrupted. I followed her and stood on the step looking down into the dark little scullery. I was going to enjoy telling my story.

"You'd never guess what happened, the tram crashed into a shop in Nelson Street - it jumped the points." Without even looking up from her task she said, " I knew that would happen one day", and she went outside into the yard. I followed.

" I'd been sitting in the front seat". I gave a dramatic sigh and waited for her to comment, but she took no notice, so I continued.

"But I'd gone back to watch the conductor change the points, good job I did else I would have been covered in broken glass."

"It's a wonder you didn't have your nose in a book, perhaps that'll teach you something." End of my adventure.

Once the family realised that I read books from the library they always saw it as something harmful. None of them belonged to the library and they never felt the need to read books; newspapers and magazines yes, but books no. Why couldn't I be like them? If you didn't conform then there must be something odd about you.

I had discovered that I was odd man out when I went to Dad to ask him to sign my enrolment form for the Public Library. He refused. It was my teacher who vouched for me, and the library became my escape from the cobbled street and the house that was either empty or occupied with people who seemed to want no part of me. They hardly spoke to me or touched me in a loving way. As a result, I sat and read and was called lazy, day-dreamer and such like, but as each member of the family went his separate way no-one realised how often I was alone. They weren't cruel; they just did not think about it. Life had always been like that and you grew up to look after yourself. Although while a child food, shelter and clothing were provided you were expected to cope for yourself as soon as possible.

I grew up when I was eleven years old. The day had started off normally, but as soon as I awoke I knew that something was going to happen, my heart was beating just that bit faster - why? It was just another school day, and we didn't break up for the summer holidays for a couple of weeks or more ... so why did I feel like this? It was like a vague foreboding, I just knew that today something exciting was going to happen. The day wore on until just before school finished when a monitor came into the room with a message that I was to go to the Headmaster's study at once. I had wings on my feet as I ran upstairs to Mr Nixon where for the next five minutes I entered my heaven on earth. The headmaster handed me the forms for my parents to sign which would enable me to go to the school of their choice within the category of the scholarship I had won, the following year.

He said he would have preferred to have met Mum and Dad to discuss it with them but as it was impossible for them to take time off from work he explained to me the advantages and disadvantages of one school against another. School uniform was obligatory and there would possibly be help if any finance was required. He would like the forms back as soon as possible before the school broke up for the summer holidays.

As I walked home and prepared tea my mind was deep in Angela Brazil country. I knew that I would not be going to a boarding school but I would have a uniform, meet new school friends and be learning and reading, which I enjoyed.

The subject of my scholarship had not been mentioned at home since the news of my award. No-one had congratulated me and I hadn't really expected them to. Once again I was being the odd man out and once the news got out even some of the women in the street looked at me strangely. Fancy, they said, fancy you going off to one of those posh schools. And they sniffed, glad that it wasn't their daughter.

I put the envelope containing the forms and other information by the side of Dad's plate, but Mum put it behind the clock saying not to worry Dad with papers until he had had his tea. I thought the meal would never end, and after tea I sat and waited for Mum to give him the papers. But she had forgotten all about them and in the end, no longer able to bear it, I got them myself and gave them to him.

He read them, and without even looking at me, tore them up and threw them in the fireplace. I couldn't believe it. I felt hot tears prickling behind my eyes.

"But Dad, it's about my scholarship, my new school, you've got to choose."

"I've chosen. You'll do the same as your sister and brother. No need for all that bloody learning after you're fourteen. In any case you won't like it, you'll beg us to take you away so as you can earn money like the rest of us. You're different from the others at those schools ... you're not meant for it ... you won't like it."

I pleaded with him but it was no use, he had torn up my dreams and thrown them away. Something snapped inside me and I attacked him, punching him in the chest and crumpling his newspaper over his stomach. He leapt from the chair, his hands automatically going to the buckle of his leather belt. If Mum had not stepped between us I would have been whipped across the face with it. She begged him to put the belt away and listen to her but it was no use, his temper had turned him into a monster, shouting abuse. I flew from the house and the street, tears pouring down my cheeks.

Every animal has its own lair and I was no exception. Long ago I had found my own secret refuge and now, unconsciously, I had gone straight to it ... on top of a hill in Greenwich Park. It was here that I sat while the sobs shook my body, as I gazed over what is to me the most beautiful panorama in the world ... the river at Greenwich, with views of the cross on the top of St Paul's and Tower Bridge on the one hand and the round-bellied gasholders of the gas-works on the other.

Slowly my sobs subsided and I was soothed by the sound of the breeze in the old fig tree behind the railings.

Gradually too there formed in my mind a plan to escape; one day I would get away from the street and everyone in it. I would not lead a life like Mum's ... nor would I live in a house like ours. I knew that night that I had left the land of childhood behind me. Never again would I look to Dad for love or companionship and Mum's world was already full to overflowing with a constant round of work to keep us all clean, well fed and shod. I was well and truly on my own.

CHAPTER ELEVEN

Mum's world was dominated by superstition and she was seriously upset by anyone or anything that brought illness, bad luck or downright evil into our lives.

Dad laughed at her but always obeyed her do's and don'ts. He loved to play cards, particularly cribbage at dinner-time at work, and sometimes in the pub, but Mum said that card packs were devils' playthings and would not allow them to be brought into our house.

I was nearly fourteen when she at last relented, and at that late age I learned to play for the first time card games like rummy and snap. By this time the second world war had started and I can only suppose that Mum imagined nothing more evil could happen to us. Anyway cards were now permissible, not only in the house but in the air raid shelter in the garden.

As a child I always seemed to be doing the wrong thing at the wrong time or on the wrong day. If it was a Friday then I must not cut my nails, and almost every day I crossed the knives or spilt the salt. And the screams I caused by putting new shoes on a table before they had been worn - I found it difficult not to when arriving back with lots of shopping which was dumped altogether on to the table.

If a picture fell off the wall then someone would die within the week. Fred took down one of our pictures and showed Mum how worn the string was. The picture did fall down a few weeks later. When Grandad died three days later Mum looked at Fred and said that would teach him not to blaspheme. She also said that in any case she had seen a mouse sitting up in the corner of the kitchen fireplace early one morning and he was singing and if that wasn't a sign of death, well!

My godmother, who lived next door, shared Mum's superstitious beliefs and also the word of the fortune teller. She persuaded Mum to visit a spiritual meeting and they both returned from this convinced that they had received messages from someone 'passed over'. Dad was angry about this and forbade Mum to go again. However he quite enjoyed my godmother's regular performance when the new moon appeared. He would stand with his hands in his pockets and laugh openly at her. As soon as she saw the new moon she went into the garden, bowed three times and turned her money over in her handbag. Aunt Dora was as she put it 'well-padded' and it was a little difficult for her to stop falling over as she bowed down, so she would have to hold on to the fence and as she pulled herself up there would be Dad grinning at her. There would be a few sharp words from Aunt Dora and Dad would come back into the kitchen with all kinds of bad luck heaped on his head, but I noticed once or twice that he kept his hands in his pocket as she bowed ... could he have been turning his money over?

Mum said it was unlucky to pass anyone on the stairs. It certainly was in our house, the stairs being narrow, dark and steep. If you did try to pass Daisy as she was coming down dressed in her new finery she would just push you back in case you dirtied her or tore her stockings. She just kept coming down, arms in front and pushing you back until you reached the bottom - and if you met Fred coming up, you just got banged against the wall as he shoved you to one side, but I suppose Mum's warnings meant more than just that. Two teaspoons in a saucer meant twins in the family of the person you handed it to; to stir with a knife meant to stir up strife. If crows were about you prayed you saw more than one - one for sorrow, two for joy. Luckily we had only sparrows and pigeons up our street ...

The one thing that puzzles me still was that Gran taught me to wet my forefinger and make the sign of the cross over my toes to arrest the onslaught of pins and needles - I always did it and the pins and needles always vanished ... even today at the first tingle my fingers automatically seek my mouth. These and many more superstitions dominated our household, rarely heralds of good luck or joy, with perhaps the exception of Mum's philosophical saying 'when one door shuts another opens'.

Indeed, as the door to a new world of education was firmly closed against me a new door did open, and I found my first really close friend. It was a friendship that was to last our lives.

CHAPTER TWELVE

Marjorie just seemed to appear when I was sitting alone on the window-sill of our front parlour unwilling to join in the games with the other children. Normally no 'foreign' children visited the top of our street since it led nowhere and the local street gang was strict about allowing strangers in our games.

From her first "hallo" I noticed how differently she spoke. She was very pretty, with dark wavy hair and her clothes were modern, the skirts quite short. Large dark eyes smiled at me from a very pale face - instantly I took to her and we started to talk.

Her father was the new manager of the grocer's on the corner of the street and they were going to live in the flat above the shop. So tight was our street community that until that moment I had not known that anyone could live above the corner premises; my eyes had never wandered above the windows displaying the cheeses and bacons. Life now opened up and I learned for the first time what it was like to be almost a part of a real family. I was accepted by Marjorie's mother and father as another daughter, which probably wasn't difficult as there were already five children in the family. Marjorie was in the middle, with a brother and sister either side of her.

I was soon spending as much time in their home as in my own, longing to join this noisy, squabbling, laughing, loving family. I thought it was a miracle that we had met, as I soon learned that their living standards had taken a tumble.

Marjorie's father had owned two businesses in London and during the winter they had lived above them. In the summer they had moved to a seaside home. The sea air had been good for Marjorie who was 'delicate' but within a short time of living in the smoky atmosphere of Greenwich she again fell ill necessitating treatment for a long part of her life.

The businesses had not prospered so Mr Wilkins had obtained a situation as manager of a store which had branches throughout London. He was an expert in all departments of the grocery and provision trade, in boning bacon, cooking ham and deftly handling the wooden butter pats. To see him scoop up a huge lump from the large golden mound and never be more than a fraction out of the required weight was something to marvel at. Marjorie was a whole year older but in her I found an ideal friend for she too loved reading, and liked music. In her I had someone to look up to and ask the hundred and one questions stored inside for so long. As soon as I had done my afternoon chores of laying the tea-table, preparing the fire and filling the kettle I would rush down the street, through the wooden gate and the tiny backyard, then with a warning shout would run up the narrow staircase leading to their flat. The wooden gate in the side wall of the shop soon became more familiar than my own front door and much more welcoming.

Once a week from the cellars came a pungent smell accompanied by clouds of greasy steam - the steam found its way up the stairs and followed you into the kitchen however quickly you opened and closed the door. Mr Wilkins was cooking the hams, the key to ensuring that this branch of the business lived up to its reputation. It might smell awful when cooking but its taste was delicious.

The kitchen was twice the size of ours as indeed were most of the rooms above the shop. But the big table that was necessary for such a large family took up almost half of the room. One wall was covered by a large dresser which not only held crockery but was usually draped with newspapers, nappies, babies' feeding bottles, books, pencils, paper, sewing, knitting and of course comics which we all read. This background symbolised their home throughout my association with it, especially the nappies and babies' feeding paraphernalia, as within the year Marjorie had another baby brother, number six to them but number one to me.

Most mothers in our street kept to the old-fashioned methods of bringing up babies; they were well hidden for the first few weeks, swathed in bundles of shawls, binders and bonnets. If it wasn't too cold they might be put outside the door in the pram, hood up and the covers pulled over half the baby's face. They were crooned over and cuddled and often spoilt for the first few months but as soon as they could sit up and take notice they were regularly put into the passage by themselves where they crawled, learned to stand and played with balls and rattles leaving Mum to get on with her housework.

In the summer a barrier of some sort would be fixed across the open front door where baby could see and be seen by all the street. Old women would slobber kisses on them as they went down the street to the shops and old men would stop and stick their fingers into little tummies, at the same time breathing tobacco fumes into their faces. And when the tradesmen's horses and carts came up the street they would gurgle with laughter or scream as the clip-clop over the cobbles drew nearer.

When Donald was born I was allowed to be present at his first bath at home. He was very blonde and as his skin was golden pink, his rounded legs and arms made him look like a cherub as he lay in his mother's lap and she soaped and rinsed him. To my delight - and fear - she gave him to me to hold and what feelings surged through me as I held this real live living doll ... I stared into his blue eyes and he looked back into mine. Mrs Wilkins said they hadn't focused yet and it would be some while before he could really see and get to know us ... but I didn't believe it; he had looked back into my eyes, we were friends.

That day I felt part of the family. I talked about nothing else at home and although Mum didn't mind Marjorie coming into our house now and again, Fred and Daisy said they were sick and tired of hearing nothing but Wilkins. Again I learned to keep quiet about my days and how I spent them. Summer for once sped by.

CHAPTER THIRTEEN

Usually time hung heavily in the summer. Most of the children in the street went away for a week or two, maybe to stay with an Aunt in London or, if they were lucky, at the seaside. But at eleven years of age I was still awaiting my first sight of the sea.

There were no paid holidays for Mum or Dad. Daisy and Fred managed a week off but I don't know if they were paid for it. Daisy never went away but Fred did go to Wales once to stay with a friend's aunt and uncle. I can remember the excitement when we received a picture of Ebbw Vale from him.

Most of my time I spent in Greenwich Park or alone by the river and although I was often alone I was rarely lonely. The gardeners always had time to talk as they dug up a new flower bed, or planted out bedding plants. Sometimes there were other children - the posh ones with nursemaids from the big houses on Blackheath who would feed bread to the ducks on the pond, or to the deer in the enclosure by the side of the Gardens.

The tennis courts outside Rangers House were usually occupied and I would sit on the grass and watch, not knowing the rules or how they scored, but fascinated by the players in their smart white outfits. I can remember sitting there and seeing the first advertising by an aeroplane; I could not believe it as the word PERSIL appeared in white across a blue sky!

Greenwich Park had plenty of visitors and foreign tourists in the summer, mostly Germans who travelled by ships which moored at Greenwich Pier. They would congregate in groups around General Wolfe's statue which stands on the top of Observatory Hill. He had lived in a house at the top of Crooms Hill which runs down the side of the Park and he stood then - as now - staring at one of the most famous panoramas of London.

This view drew me like a magnet and still does, and although some prefer to look at it from the Isle of Dogs, I like to have my feet on Greenwich soil and look towards London one way, and follow the Thames running down to the sea in the other direction.

Turner painted many scenes of the Thames and the chair he sat on can be seen today in St Mary's Church, Battersea, but his favourite spot was Greenwich and his picture 'The Fighting Temeraire' shows the stretch of river flowing past the Naval College, where the Cutty Sark now stands in dry dock. The poet Samuel Rogers wrote about Greenwich Hospital and illustrated it with a view from the Isle of Dogs ... even Mary Shelley managed to bring Greenwich into her famous story of Frankenstein ! I was rarely lonely in my wanderings around Greenwich ... the whole world was there.

We children played games along the Meridian Line ... walking along it with our eyes shut and shouting out that we could walk through the middle of the world without looking.

The river at Greenwich had two small beaches and good use was made of them by mothers and children on warm summer days for picnics and the construction of muddy sandcastles. We paddled and swam too, despite the strong currents found on this stretch of the river, where every year at least one child drowned. Beachcombing was something that attracted me, especially after Gran had taken Old Bill as a lodger. He was a well-known Greenwich character whom most mothers told their children to avoid. All the year Old Bill could be found walking along the riverside, poking amongst the rubbish, to retrieve bits of metal, old nails, coins and anything else that took his fancy.

Grandad had been sent to the institute which was part of the workhouse following an accident at the gas works. When Gran visited him she often found Old Bill sitting by his bed talking to him, so after Grandad died and his pension ceased Gran decided to take in a lodger. So Old Bill left the workhouse and came to live at Gran's, handing over his old age pension to her each week and in return getting two shillings back as spending money.

He was a plump, jolly man, with a round, red face which shone as if polished. Each day he wore the one dark grey suit given him by the workhouse. His room in Gran's house was as neat and tidy as himself. Gran of course cleaned out the room once a week when she did the rest of the house but she was not allowed to touch the round table set in the corner by the window, upon which Bill set out his special treasures found on the beach, in the park or in the streets. There were piles of safety pins, drawing pins, nails, foreign coins, brooches, beads and something I coveted most of all - a tiny pen-knife with a mother-of-pearl handle and two small blades. There was also a copy of the Bible only two inches square but although the metal covers were still perfect the pages were spoilt by river water. There were pieces of metal which had been twisted into shapes that satisfied Bill's artistic sense and branches of wood which he said 'felt right'. He often let me accompany him on these walks when he would tell me about the different ships en route to London; the Swedish timber boats and the cable boats tying up at the factory near Blackwall Reach before going out to the Atlantic Ocean to lay the cable on the sea bed.

I learned so much from him that when the London County Council held an exhibition of children's work my scrap book of the River Thames and its traffic was given a place on the stands erected in County Hall - but none of us went to see the exhibits as Dad thought it a waste of time and money.

But from Old Bill I acquired a life-time interest in rivers, canals and boats. It should have come from Dad, for I learned years afterwards that our family had a tradition of boat-building back to at least 1700. Grandfather had had his own barge-yard at Brentford for a short time until he had drank the profits away. I also knew that my great-grandfather had worked in Rotherhithe as one of Brunel's workmen on the

Great Eastern. In addition I found out how Dad got his nickname of Dolly by which he was known throughout his life to the watermen of Greenwich and Charlton.

The youngest of five brothers, all apprenticed to the boat building trade, Dad was very small and his mother decided he was delicate but she was over-ruled by her husband. At fourteen when he was told to report to the barge-yard for work, his mother dressed him in a velvet suit with lace cuffs hoping this would show up his slight figure and short stature. The workmen burst into laughter and shouted that "a dolly had come to work in the yard". His father was furious and made the boy start work immediately dressed as he was, so Dad decided to show them that he was as good as any of them. Sure enough he proved himself at his trade until he was seventy, still called, but now affectionately, Dolly.

He worked on several barges that are now in the Maritime Museum and advised on the handling of the Cutty Sark before she was brought up from Greenhithe to her dry dock at Greenwich. Despite this background he thought it a waste of time to talk about the river, see exhibitions or even pass on information to his children, with the one exception of my brother Fred.

His pride showed in his thin features the day he apprenticed Fred as a barge-builder at a barge-yard adjacent to the one in which he worked.

When I brought home pieces of old ships' timber I'd found on the beach he would give them a glance but say nothing. Imagine my surprise after his death to learn that he had been given pieces of the old Waterloo Bridge by his boss and asked to carve them into miniatures as souvenirs for various privileged people. And never one did he bring home to show us.

After I grew up and began to write and broadcast I originated several pieces about the river and my biggest thrill came after interviewing Commander West on the Cutty Sark, when he asked me to sign the visitor's book which Prince Philip had used ! Dad was still alive and my first thought was to rush home and tell him but his only comment was that it was a pity they had demolished The Ship public house to make the dry dock for the Cutty Sark. In fact the pub had been bombed during the war, but as far as he was concerned the site was The Ship.

Cold wet summer days tended to drag and usually I'd go round and see Gran whom I was not allowed to visit until I'd had my dinner as Mum did not want Gran to think I only went for a meal. Sometimes Gran would be making pastry and I would be allowed to make a jam tart, or she might be just working on one of her rag rugs, using pieces of coloured cloth which she wove in and out of a large piece of hessian. She would talk about her childhood in Bures, Suffolk, where she had worked in the fields with her father from the age of five, and how her mother would hide her beneath her voluminous skirts if she had misbehaved to save her from a beating from her father. Even in those days her father Daniel had had a name as a rough, hard man.

She remembered having toothache and her father took her along to the local inn where she was given some brandy to swallow before the innkeeper pulled out the offending tooth.

She also recalled how her father had slipped on to his scythe, practically severing his thumb. He had returned home with a dockleaf wrapped around it and when this turned black with blood he sent Gran out for more dockleaves and a spider's web. With the web inside the leaves he had tied this round his thumb and Gran said that when the leaves had withered the thumb was grafted back on as good as new. I loved hearing these stories and didn't care if they were true or false, but if I showed surprise she would immediately slap me and say it was God's own truth she was telling.

Once her father had to visit London where he had a sister who had been taken ill. Daniel's employer was a kindly man and besides allowing him a day off from work, lent him a horse and trap in which to travel to the station before boarding the train for London. For some reason he decided to take his daughter with him and Gran remembered her shock on seeing so many people in the streets. The shops were so much larger than she had ever imagined and the horse-buses went so fast. She was taken for a walk in Battersea Park before returning home, and thought all the women out walking must be the Queen, or at least princesses, because they wore such lovely hats.

CHAPTER FOURTEEN

The summer I met Marjorie was the time I discovered just how exciting a grocer's could be. Mr Wilkins allowed us to wander about, so long as we didn't get in the way of the staff when they were serving. The shop had three counters, one on each side and one across the back. I can recall only two of the staff being female, one was Peggy the egg girl, who worked outside. Large trestles piled high with eggs stood on the pavement where Peggy deftly put dozens and half dozens into paper bags, for in those days they were not sold in boxes as now. Breakages occurred and these eggs were sold separately at a lower price. Most of us in the street bought half a dozen good ones and half a dozen cracked at a time.

Peggy was extremely pretty and, like my sister, copied the film stars, but she was softer and daintier, her hair curling down to her shoulders in natural waves, unlike the rigid crimping effect produced by tongs, or the sausage curls of the permanent waving machine. Even in overalls, which she wore wrapped tightly around her figure, she did not look like a shop girl, and Mr Wilkins had his work cut out trying to stop the young men from wasting her time. But he could not stop the policeman who stood on the corner of the street every morning, at dinner time and again in the afternoon because he was there to help the children cross over the busy main road to the school behind the church. Even when it rained Peggy stayed outside in a black shiny raincoat over her overall, with the blinds pulled over the egg stands. Her speech was better than ours and as she lived near the top of Vanburgh Hill near Blackheath it is possible she came from a better-off family.

Marjorie thought Peggy was marvellous and they became very friendly, which caused me pangs of jealousy, but I was still too enthralled with the newness of my association for this to last. There was always someone to play with or talk to and the new baby constantly needed someone to push him out in his pram. Naturally by mixing with them it wasn't long before I was copying their way of speaking, or at least trying to pronounce my words correctly.

The other member of the shop staff who talked to us frequently was Molly, the cashier. She sat in a small square box situated in the middle of the shop floor. When you had bought your provisions you took a slip of paper with the price on it to Molly, as no money was handed over the counter to the shop assistants. Molly spiked the slips which were added up at the end of the day. How she deciphered some of the writing, especially on busy weekends, when a hurriedly pencilled three-farthings could be a farthing or a halfpenny, I don't know. Ledgers had to be balanced and on Saturdays when the shop remained open until about ten at night it must have been quite late when she returned home. The best thing about Molly's job I thought was that she had a telephone beside her. It was an upright one with a separate ear-piece hanging by its side but to my bitter disappointment I was never allowed to use it. Molly was always there by its side, waiting to pick it up and speak magically to someone miles away. How I longed to use a telephone - what an adventure it would be!

The closing time on Saturdays depended on how quickly the butcher sold off the joints of meat he had cut. Around eight o'clock he would start bringing the prices down and as the window on his side of the shop opened up from the bottom, he could come out onto the pavement and unhook a joint off the rail in the window with his long pole before selling at the lower prices. Most of the women in the street waited until then before buying the Sunday dinner.

Even when Molly reached home she had not finished work for the day. She lived in New Cross where her mother kept a boarding-house for the music hall artists who appeared at the New Cross Empire, whose suppers Molly had to help serve.

Through Molly I started to take an interest in show-biz people and when I was given an autograph book as a birthday present she often took it home with her and obtained many famous signatures for me. I treasured that book and was very proud to see such famous names as Harry Lauder, Sid Plummer, Ronald Chesney, Hutch, Turner and Layton, and many more, sadly all lost during a bombing raid in the second world war.

The male members of the shop put up with us hanging about and asking questions, but never became particularly friendly; to me they all looked alike in their long white aprons and white coats. The meat, bacon, butter and cheese counters were made of marble and the floor was a black and white terrazo, all scrubbed every morning and clean sawdust thrown down on the butchery side.

The meat was delivered at the small side gate and taken into the back room where each carcass was weighed before it was put in the refrigerator. Sometimes when they had finished unloading they would lift Marjorie and me up and we would cling to the weighing hook and watch the needle move round. As both of us were slightly built the butcher said together we wouldn't even make a good Irish stew.

Marjorie's eldest brother worked on the bacon counter. He was being trained to be a number-one bacon hand and I thought he was marvellous as he boned a side of bacon, his long razor sharp knife gliding through the pink flesh, curving around the bone and quickly nipping off any fat or rind that wasn't required. I learned the names of the different cuts and was pleased when he said that my Mum was wise to buy streaky rashers as they were the best flavour and as good as gammon but cheaper because of the cut and size.

It wasn't very often that a customer asked for the rind to be cut off as this could be used separately to make a bacon and onion dumpling. We always bought green rather than smoked bacon on which Mum left the rind when cooking. As Dad didn't like rind I always had his and if there was anyone who did not want the rind cooked then it would be cut off and one of the toddlers would have it to chew on. It was a common sight to see children running up and down the street chewing a bacon rind.

The butter counter also sold margarine, but even in our household we bought butter to use on brown bread on Sundays. The butter stood in round golden domes, some wrapped and weighed, but mostly the customer liked to see her butter deftly scooped up with the two wooden pats and banged and turned into a neat block before being put on the scale. A final touch with the pat decorated it with a cut-out thistle, which was the company trademark, and the butter was wrapped in a piece of greaseproof paper before going into a bag, which also had the thistle on it. On busy days you could hear the clatter of the butter pats as they banged together and then went back on to the marble counter. I was allowed to try just once and was surprised to find how heavy they were.

The thistle trade mark became the bane of many a mum's life, for it wasn't long before most children found out that if you stood a cup of tea or a jug of hot water on top of the bag the thistle would come off like a transfer. As most of our scullery tables were covered in American oil-cloth which was a shiny washable material this was the first place that experiments were made. You placed the bag face down onto the table, put the hot teapot on it for a few minutes and there was a lovely purple thistle.

Alongside the butter counter were the cheeses, covered in thin cloths which in summer were wrung out in bowls of cold water kept beneath the counter. This stopped the cheese sweating too much. There were no refrigerated counters in the shops then and on hot days most of the meat was kept in the back room fridge and brought out as required.

Like the bacon, cheese rind was much appreciated by the children. When I was old enough to be made responsible for the weekly grocery shopping I was told the cheese must have its rind on as it kept better and if I could not see the right piece already cut on the counter then I was to ask the assistant to take a new piece from the main cheese and slice off a wedge with the rind on. The rough criss-crossed rind, marked with the weave of the cloth, stood solid and firm against the smooth interior and none was smoother inside than the Dutch cheese standing in crimson globes. Next to that, a crumbly red Cheshire. We ate a lot of cheese and had it almost every day either in sandwiches for dinner or on toast for tea.

The counter along the back of the shop was the general grocery counter and it was here that you could sit on a chair in front of the counter, smelling the tea, coffee, pepper, curry and spices, while waiting to be served. Sugar was wrapped in blue cones of paper, and still sold loose if required. I felt smug when I too learned how to twist the blue paper into cones, but unfortunately I never did find out how to fold the top so that the sugar didn't spill. Great piles of blue sugar paper pre-cut into squares was stacked behind the counter next to the sugar sacks; the assistants seemed able to do everything in a trice; take up the scoop, weigh the sugar, twist the cone, pour in the sugar and secure the top.

There were also sacks of dried fruit, sultanas, raisins and currants, and tea was sold loose too although you could buy it in packets. Gran would not buy any tea she couldn't see as she suspected the packets probably contained sweepings from the floor!

Coffee was an unknown taste to me until the war when Mum started to buy bottles of Camp Coffee which did not wean me from my preference for strong, sweet tea. One of our most frequent purchases was condensed milk; this grey looking sweet mass was heaped into tea, spread on bread and even used to sweeten custards. Fresh milk was used only at weekends and then mainly for custards. The grocers also sold biscuits and cakes, tinned goods, jellies and jams. I spent so much time in and around the shop that I began to look upon it as mine. I would look up the street to see if anyone noticed me approaching the side gate, and if there was I would let myself in, nose-in-the-air and shut the gate with a bang as much as to say, here am I this side of the wall, but you are out there in the street on the other side.

Once upstairs with the family I would forget my airs and graces, so marvellous was it to have someone to come home and talk to. Mrs Wilkins seemed interested in the children's chatter although sometimes she would ask a question which showed that she wasn't really listening all the time, but then I would realise it was impossible with four or five of us all talking at once. She would sit there smiling, soothing the tired baby or settling an argument about whose painting brush it was, when her husband would come upstairs for his tea. Our playthings would then be pushed to one end of the table while someone put out cups and saucers, for we would all have a cup.

How I loved those afternoons. Mum said that I ought to feel sorry for Marjorie because she always had a baby in a pram to tag around with her when she went out to play but no matter how hard I tried she never understood why I spent so much time in their overcrowded flat. Before that dream summer ended I had even better luck for Marjorie told me that she was coming to my elementary school at Halstow Road. Although her father was willing to pay the fees for the Charlton Central School the doctor had decided that Marjorie's health would not stand the journey each day, and that it would be best for her to attend Halstow Road where she could go home for a midday meal.

It was with relief I heard this news, for ever since Dad's refusal to let me take up the scholarship, I had been dreading going to the elementary school. The children in the street taunted me a few times once they knew I would still be going to school with them after the summer holidays, but now I didn't mind as I had my best friend to accompany me.

CHAPTER FIFTEEN

When Daisy married I looked forward to having a bed and a room to myself. Up till then my books were piled on the floor on my side of the bedroom, and my diary as well as my poems hidden in the one drawer that Daisy allowed me for my underclothes, socks and hankies.

Now she was gone I had the front bedroom to myself. Before the week was out I summoned enough courage to ask Dad if he could make me some kind of small table for writing. To my dismay he told me that at the weekend I was to move into the small bed in the alcove in their bedroom where Fred slept. He was now to have the front bedroom. I suppose this was in fact only fair, as Fred was nearly nineteen and was now earning money and buying smart new clothes which had to be crushed in the wardrobe along with Mum's dresses and Dad's suits.

Our sleeping habits broke all kinds of Board of Health regulations throughout most of my childhood, but with only two bedrooms and Mum's refusal to turn her front parlour into sleeping quarters we had to make do with what we could.

So Fred moved to the front bedroom and I to the small bed behind the curtain at the side of Mum's bed. Fred and I hit it off quite well and he realised how upset I was. Even without my asking him he let me keep my books in his room, but I was not to go in without his permission. Mum had a large wooden ottoman at the bottom of her bed and in this we kept the bed linen, blankets and tablecloths. During Bank Holidays and Christmas, when the shops shut for a few days, we kept our bread inside the ottoman, wrapped in a linen pillowcase. If bread was brought still hot from the baker's, and wrapped in linen it kept as new for at least three or four days.

Mum told me I could have a corner of the ottoman for my underclothes and socks, but I was in despair about my diary. It was of course a secret from the family although I let Marjorie read excerpts from it sometimes.

I searched the house without success for a hiding place and finally in desperation hid it beneath my clothes in the ottoman. I made it my job to take out the clean linen every week, and to put away the freshly ironed laundry.

I was to share that bedroom for just over two years and throughout that time never became accustomed to Dad coming home under the weather or 'a little worse for wear' as he put it next day.

He was rarely violently drunk as the money was not available for heavy drinking, but now and again he'd meet up with some old cronies whom he would join on a pub crawl. He would stagger into the room swearing as he fumbled to undo his tie. Mum would sshh him several times reminding him I was in the room but he would continue until at last he had managed to climb into bed, still wearing pants and vest. He wore pyjamas only during his last days in hospital.

Sometimes I'd lie and listen to the noise coming from their bed, the heaving and moving of bodies, the murmurs, cursing, coughing and eventually the heavy breathing as sleep overtook them. In the morning I would wake to the stale air hung with beer fumes, stepping over Dad's trousers, socks and shoes as they lay in untidy heaps on the floor.

On the occasions when he was incapable of climbing our stairs Mum would leave him in his armchair in the kitchen to sleep it off. I always heard him come upstairs in the early hours of the morning. We had no electricity and he would walk around in the dark, knocking into the furniture to the accompaniment of oaths until sleep reclaimed him for the few hours left until morning.

He had two accidents while drunk, both at home. One could have been serious. He had invited friends to supper and I could hear them in the kitchen which was beneath the back bedroom. They were laughing, singing and talking when I heard Mum scream and Dad start to swear. There was silence that seemed to last for ever as I sat up in bed, ears straining. I leapt out of bed and ran downstairs. Dad was leaning against the mantelpiece with blood shooting upwards from his hand, his thumb was hanging limply. Mum came in from the scullery with a teacloth wrung out in cold water which he snatched from her and wrapped it around the thumb and wrist. He blundered towards the door with the help of one of the men. Although we lived within five minutes walk from St Alphege's Hospital he refused to go there, shouting to Mum in a thick slurry voice that he was river born and bred and was off to the Seamen's Hospital. He stumbled out of the front door, the blood pouring down his trousers.

Seamen's Hospital or more correctly The Dreadnought was well over half a mile away in West Greenwich. Somehow he made his way on foot while clutching the blood-soaked tea towel round his hand and leaning against his friend.

Next morning he returned sober, with his hand neatly bandaged. He had lost an enormous amount of blood having partially cut into an artery and yet he went to work losing only a few hours of his time. He was not allowed sick pay by his firm and lost money for time spent at the hospital or doctor's. Within three weeks or so he was able to use his hand again, thumb included.

His second accident he treated as a great joke. After a day's drinking he tried to climb the stairs only to fall back, slipping on the shiny lino as he landed back in the passage. He tried again and this time Mum and I heard him get nearer to the top when he collapsed and fell to the bottom. We found him sitting up against the passage wall, cursing Mum because the lino was too slippery. We pushed him on his hands and knees almost to the top but we could not get him over the last step onto the landing. By this time he was hunched up and almost asleep. We could move him no further so left him draped across the landing hoping he would be all right.

In the night I heard a tearing sound and next morning saw that he had torn up the lino square from the landing to cover himself with. He thought it funny when he woke up. He said he had thought he was in bed and had pulled the blanket round him. Once again he had no ill effects from the fall, the knocks on the head or the drinking.

CHAPTER SIXTEEN

A stranger to our street was immediately identifiable, although we had our regular callers whom we virtually assimilated ... the delivery men, the door-to door salesmen and the street entertainers.

No cars visited our cul-de-sac and few deliveries were made by van, so we children could play in comparative safety, sitting in the gutters and hitting our balls down the middle of the road. Our only deterrent was the grumpy old man dozing in an armchair on the doorstep.

Mum would not buy bread from the roundsman so I had to get it from Smith's the baker's which stood just around the corner and two doors down from the pub. We bought an unsliced loaf for the dinner-time sandwiches taken to work by Mum, Dad, Daisy and Fred, and a large cottage loaf for tea. Knowing what time the bread came out of the oven I always bought it hot. The temptation to prise up the top half of the cottage loaf and pick at the 'baker's kiss' as the soft doughy bit between the two halves was called, was often too much for me and I'd walk back up the street pulling at the warm white bread, hoping that Mum would not notice. Another baker, just past Blackwall Lane, displayed large trays of mince in his window and we bought halfpenny pieces of this sugary pastry filled with dried fruit on our way to school. It was supposed to be for our milk break, but as most of us had breakfasted on tea and bread we ate it long before we were supposed to.

Two milkmen delivered to our street, Mr Reid who lived two streets away and Tommy who had a small dairy in Christchurch street. Mum would buy only from Tommy as Mr Reid kept his milk churns in the passage of his house, which she felt must be quite unhygienic.

Tommy had a dairy where you could buy milk, eggs, cheese and cartons of cream. He delivered with a little grey horse hitched to a cart in the back of which stood his churn polished and gleaming with two scoops hanging over the edge.

You could buy milk scooped from the churn into your own jug or in bottles with cardboard lids. For years we preferred our own jug but gradually Mum decided that having a bottle left on the doorstep was more convenient. As more people followed suit Tommy stopped bringing the churn.

In retrospect it seems likely that both Tommy and Mr Reid obtained their milk from the same source but I had no idea how milk got into churns or bottles as I had never seen a farm and I did not know where their supplies came from. There were a few farms in Sidcup and New Eltham as I discovered later which may have been the source.

The ice-cream man was the kids' star attraction. He rode up and down the street, on his navy blue and white tricycle, ringing his bell and we would rush out to buy, for a halfpenny, creamy triangle shaped confections, which we pushed up through the cardboard container and sucked slowly to make our halfpenny investment last as long as possible. Cornets or wafers we bought only from the short, fat Italian at his pitch outside the Maze Hill Park gates. On Sundays he brought his cart up the street and when we heard his shout we would run out with basins, dishes and glasses to have filled with a big wooden spoon from his brass ice-cream tub.

His ice-cream was thick, yellow and creamy and we sometimes had it as a special treat for Sunday tea. To our amusement Gran would blow on it before she ate it, it was too cold otherwise she said.

The cat's meat man was my special friend and he too had a tricycle. He didn't call out but rang the bell and at the first ping all the cats in the street knew who he was. They would circle him mewing, crying and shoving each other out of the way as he turned and stopped outside our house where he would open the top of the bike and pull back the flaps of the lids. The strong smell of horse-flesh drove the cats wild. Inside were slices of meat on skewers, which were the regular orders, but for those of us who only bought the meat as a special treat for our pets he would take out a huge wet red slab of flesh, place on the flap and with a dangerous looking knife quickly carve off lumps which would be sliced and threaded onto a skewer after being weighed on a tiny scale.

The cats always got a few trimmings thrown amongst them and they would spit and squabble over these until one of them could see his mistress walking back to her house. Immediately he would leave the throng and follow her, certain she had his dinner. None of us had to call our cats away; instinctively they knew when we had been served. My Sandy was as greedy as the rest but as the cat's meat man stopped by our house he never jostled round the cart but sat almost disdainfully on his own doorstep until I had been handed my skewer. He would then jump up and walk beside me to the scullery at the end of the passage and his saucer by the side of the copper.

If I teased him with it he would jump onto the copper and narrow his eyes at me, but I didn't keep him waiting long as he looked forward to his special Saturday meal. Other days he had scraps, bread and milk, fish heads and bones from the rabbit legs which he gnawed clean and then discarded.

As well as delivery men visiting the street there were plenty of other callers, some to entertain and others to tempt us to buy their goods, but both gleaned little from us for their efforts.

The entertainers who came regularly were the street singers. Sometimes a man came on his own and walked up and down, cap in hand singing ballads, and on other occasions we had a young woman with a little girl who would hold tightly to the woman's hand while she sang and came round with a collecting box afterwards.

All the children looked forward most of all to the two men with the barrel organ, one dressed as a woman in a long flowing tea-gown, his head adorned with a wig of vivid orange curls, who would stand on the kerb and put on lipstick and powder. The pair would stand in the middle of the street and play the organ and sing and the woman danced up and down the street, knocking on doors or calling to upstairs windows when the curtains moved. We children would stand and clap, dancing alongside and pleading to turn the handle of the organ, or the pointer to chose the next song. Never once were we allowed to touch it and if a daring boy tried to grab the handle he would soon get a box around the ears either from the man or the woman. The make-up and gown were really grotesque, almost clown-like in appearance and not a bit feminine but we didn't mind and it was even funnier if she tripped over her long skirts and fell.

The women in the street would stand and watch from their doorsteps, some making remarks as the woman passed, and others would go indoors with their children banging the door behind them. They would say it wasn't right to see a man like that, but I could stand and stare as long as I wanted to because Mum was at work and I had no-one to stop me. It was the one time when the other children envied me.

The one caller Mum saw was the very old Indian who occasionally came on a Saturday afternoon when he could be sure of a sale from our Daisy, who could not resist buying one of his bright long scarves or some ribbon.

He was fat and elderly with a large bushy beard and a towering pleated turban. He wore long skirts covered by a coat which reached to his knees and a cummerbund round the waist. In his hand he clutched a large, battered brown suitcase which he placed on the doorstep and had open by the time you came to the door. Inside the case was a glittering display of silks, scarves, ivory combs, brooches, ribbons, veils, needles, cottons and pins. The colours stood out gaily against the grey background of the street and, even if it was a weekday and Mum was at work, the display would be shown to me alone. I would stand and look down at the brilliance at my feet while the Indian peered past me down our passage to see if there was anyone else in the house who might buy. Eventually he would sigh, close the case and patiently go next door to start the show again. He spoke little English, but would trickle the materials through his fingers like a coloured waterfall, all the time smiling and nodding while mumbling gently under his breath.

Unwelcome weekly visitors were the rent collectors. The houses were owned by various individuals or small estate companies. Ours was owned by Black and Daniels and they had half a dozen properties in the street and the Grove. Generally we were good tenants and the rent was ready on Monday mornings, but there were a couple of families where the collector would have to wait for his money as food came first. One such family had numerous children and a permanently exhausted mother who wore her hair scraped back with grips from her thin peaky face. There were constant fights and rows in the house and frequently as you passed the front door you had to duck quickly as a milk bottle or jug was thrown at a fleeting boy or even the mother herself.

The husband spent a good deal of time out of work or in prison and the mother would have to rely on money from the Relief, but most of the women in the street including Mum saw that the children never went hungry and the remains of stews and puddings were sent along to the grateful woman.

Her family increased yearly and eventually the local Authorities decided that some of the older children would have to be cared for in a children's home. It was obvious that the poor woman was beyond the point of realising that her children were not being looked after, fed properly or even being washed and dressed decently enough for them to go to school.

When the time came for the children to go, the eldest boy and girl who were about eleven and twelve refused to leave their mother. After much arguing and to-ing and fro-ing by the Authorities, they were left with the mother, a family unit again. The street backed up the decision as it was apparent that the children loved their mother and she them. From then on the eldest boy and girl ran the house with the help of the other women in the street.

The woman's mother who lived nearby came round regularly and eventually the husband, who up to that time spent so little of his life in the street he was almost a stranger, became a reformed character when the coming of the Second World War meant work for everyone.

Besides collecting money the rent collectors took many complaints as well. Most of the houses were very old and lacked many of the modernisations possessed by other houses. Every winter rain leaked through our back bedroom ceiling and often the outside lavatory failed to work properly.

Mum coveted a deep white porcelain sink instead of our shallow yellow stone one, which was only about three inches deep, but was never given one.

We were constantly told that improvements were coming to the street and one day we were told that the first phase was scheduled for the following month. Would it be an indoor lavatory? Would we have a hot water system? or even electricity? Great was everyone's disappointment when all that happened was that the street name was changed, which left us wondering how it had improved us. Now we were no longer Woodland Street, but Woodland Walk. We had to wait another three years for the second improvement - electricity. The indoor lavatory and bathroom never arrived, not even twenty years later. The street had regular daily visitors who did not live there or deliver to us. These were the people who sold fruit and used the small sheds erected in alley-ways and odd corners to store their stalls and produce.

Among these was Ben, a round rosy man looking like one of his shiny red apples. His stall was one of the first to be trundled over the cobbles every morning, with his boxes of apples and oranges rocking perilously until he reached his corner pitch. The majority of the streets had stalls on the corner, some had five or six stalls up the street itself. As our street not only had cobbles but was very narrow, we had just one stall, which sold salad items and was owned by a slim wiry man, with thick black curly hair.

He looked like a gypsy, but spoke in a soft whispery voice, quite unlike the usual stall-holders who shouted their wares. The salad stall was not much larger than a barrow, the sort pushed by two hands, and it was seldom lit on dark nights by the naphtha flares which the proper stalls fixed to the corner posts. The salad man kept his stall in a corrugated iron lean-to on a waste piece of ground at the top of our street and it was here that he cooked the beetroots in an old copper over a fire in the open air. The steamy sweet smell of cooking beets greeted me most mornings when I went outside to the lavatory. On Fridays Mum would send me round to him before he laid out the stall and I would buy the beets all hot and soft, and wrapped in newspaper. We kept ours in the scullery on top of our copper where years of storage had marked the white wooden lid with patches of red as the juice seeped through the paper.

The salad stall was laid out like a work of art and Larry, the owner took time and pride over it each morning. Cos lettuces were cut through the middle and the two halves placed side by side, the curly edges of the leaves showing the darker green fading to paler yellowy green deep inside the lettuce. Cabbage lettuce were displayed like green roses at the top of the stall and crimson radish globes were bundled and washed before they were grouped against the lettuce. Cucumbers were always left in a box and you helped yourself but spring onions shining from the water they had been swished around in to release the dirt from their roots were bundled together with rafia and lay along the bottom of the stall. When tomatoes were in season they were given a centre display, heaped in a perilous mountain which looked ready to topple any minute.

If a coal cart came back early from its round the salad stall had to be pushed round into the main road to give the horse and cart enough room to turn into the street. Much shouting and swearing went on if that happened on a bad day when Larry's tomatoes were still piled high. Once the stall was back in its place he'd roll another cigarette and sit on his upturned apple box by the side of the stall slitting newspapers in half, stacking them in neat piles under the stall.

On Saturdays his son would help him, tying radishes and onions in bundles, cutting lettuces and learning the art of the display from his dad. Where they came from I never knew but throughout the whole of my street life they were there even on cold winter days when the stall only boasted beetroots and cabbages.

CHAPTER SEVENTEEN

A gas lamp stood at the corner of the street and the alley leading to the Grove, and a second at the top of the street, by our house. When I was very young the lamps were still tended by a lamplighter who, with his long pole, unlatched the glass door at the top and, to my entranced eyes, made the gas mantle start to glow. The street was softened in the yellow glow from the gaslight and when it was bedtime there was no need to light the gas bracket above the mantlepiece as the whole room took on a pink or green tint, depending on whether the summer or winter curtains were up.

The disappearance of the lamplighter and the arrival of automatic gas lamps was really the first modernisation in the street, but we had to wait until 1937 for electricity.

Fred immediately asked Dad if we could have a wireless set. Up to now Dad had been opposed to anything associated with wires, batteries and accumulators and although there was a family in the Grove and some of Fred's friends with wirelesses we were still waiting for this new invention to invade our family life. Dad was quite content without electricity or a wireless and he could not understand why we were so excited. Eventually he let himself be persuaded that it would do no harm and he agreed that we could have it. There would be little disruption in the house while the wiring was installed which was just as well as he hated any distraction from his regular routines. Eagerly we awaited the great day when the workmen would arrive to dig a trench up our street. The work would take about three or four days according to a notice we had received, but the authorities had reckoned without our cobbles, and it was long after this time before the cables were laid. The street then returned back to normal, apart from a wide black ribbon of asphalt running down the street. This delay and the scarring of the street brought forth much comment from Dad and we hoped that when the electricians started wiring the house Dad would not be around. But we need not have worried, for he had decided to have no contact with anyone from the electricity company. If the men were still around when he came home from work he retreated to the pub as soon as tea was over. He allowed us to have only one point installed which was in the kitchen. With a multi-plug we could run our wireless and an electric iron as well. As it turned out Mum was never happy with it and soon reverted to her old flat irons heated on the gas-stove in the scullery.

We had no other points but we had electric light in the kitchen, front parlour, and two bedrooms. The scullery had nothing but a candle if I felt frightened of the dark. This was the maximum electricity Dad said we could afford.

As the houses were so small the electricians found great difficulty in siting the meters and fuse boxes; in our case the only place was beneath the bottom shelf of the food cupboard in the kitchen.

This cupboard, six feet high and two feet wide, stood against a wall on one side matched by another cupboard to hold our coal on the other. To get to the meter and fuses necessitated kneeling and peering under the lower shelf which was about eighteen inches from the floor. Eventually all problems were overcome and the day came when we put our sixpences in the slot and switched on.

It was like firework night in the street. We popped into each other's houses to see the effect, noticing how the bright light showed up faded wallpaper, stained distemper walls and cracked ceilings that the gas light had camouflaged with its soft shadows.

One family kept the street door open all the evening to show off their bare electric bulb glowing in the passage as this was a real luxury, not many of us had one in this part of the house. Before leaving us the electricians gave advice on changing fuses and of course Dad ran true to form by insisting that it was all bloody common-sense and refusing to listen.

Fred however had spent a lot of time with the workmen and listened intently.

At the end of the month Dad put down a deposit on our first wireless set, a Cossor which was bought from a shop in Trafalgar Road. We found room for a small bamboo table to stand against the wall by the kitchen window near the point and the wireless became the pride of the family.

We loved it and listened continuously. After school I rushed home to prepare tea and then listen to Children's Hour - Uncle Mac, Uncle David - whom I felt were actually speaking to me. I gave them faces, bodies, dressed them and knew them as real friends. Mum loved the music programmes and to everyone's surprise Dad became quite a fan of the dance bands that played in the evenings. Dad and I started having guessing games as to which pianist was playing on Saturday evenings, when a quarter of an hour was given to a well-known artist. I developed a good ear for personal styles of playing and could soon recognise Billy Mayerl, Carrol Gibbons and the two duettists, Ivor Moreton and Dave Kaye, after only a few bars. We graduated to dance orchestras and knew immediately if it was Ambrose ... Roy Fox ... Harry Roy or Geraldo. Dad and I had great fun on these guessing games.

Then the day we had all been dreading came, a fuse blew and it happened on a late Saturday afternoon when Fred was at a dog track. Dad said he knew what to do and with his tool box was soon on his knees grunting and swearing as he tried to open the fuse box. Mum and I hovered behind him until he said we were blocking the light when we retreated behind the kitchen table. Dad red in the face surfaced for a moment, and grabbed the pair of pincers - there was a crack and a blue flash shot from the cupboard sending Dad crashing into the table which tipped up knocking Mum and me against the wooden partition. Outside we heard voices shouting in the street and I ran to the front door. Bewildered residents of all ages were running up and down the street and it soon became apparent that we were not the only house without electricity - Dad had cut the main cable and fused every house in the street.

As it was nearly six o'clock and a Saturday at that, no electrician would come until Monday so gas lit all our houses that weekend. As Dad came out of the pub on Sunday night and walked up the street he said it looked more like home to him than it had ever done since the bleedin' electric came.

CHAPTER EIGHTEEN

About three times a year the gypsies descended on the street, some of the women heavily shawled and with babies slung on their backs. They carried large baskets of pegs, combs, bunches of flowers and lucky charms which were like corn dollies but made of twigs with pieces of wire twisted through them.

Women felt uncomfortable when the gypsies came and the children were told that a gypsy would get them if they were naughty. I was instructed not to wander on to Blackheath as it was there they made their camps and they might put a curse on us if we went too near to them.

The gypsy women came on Saturday afternoons and Mum always bought something to avoid their curse; as a result we were blessed and promised a flow of wealth through life simply because we bought their dollypegs. If Daisy was home she always bought paper flowers which we put in a vase on the kitchen mantlepiece. Fresh flowers however were displayed in our front parlour window for all to see, the aspidastra being relegated while the flowers lasted. I wished we could grow flowers in our back yard like Mr Dalton next door but no-one bothered about it and we just had a few radishes one year when I bought a packet of seeds. We also had a ramshackle shed where Dad kept tins of paint with rusty lids and a few tools. The only plants were a Virginia Creeper on the yard wall which turned into a riot of red leaves in the autumn and some sunflowers which had seeded themselves and grew at the back of the shed providing seeds for the parrot.

Sometimes the gypsy offered to tell fortunes and there was a ready customer in Aunt Dora who would promptly tell Mum the marvellous things forecast for her future and ever more wonderful the events the gypsy knew had happened in the past. Aunt Dora loved fortune telling and she was told on one occasion that she would have two husbands and the second marriage would not be as happy as the first. Dad was furious when he heard about this as Uncle Dave, a quiet gentle man, was still very much alive and healthy. He ticked off Aunt Dora and told Mum she should not listen to such rubbish. Mum was concerned about this prediction and you could almost see her sigh of relief when Uncle Dave returned safely each night from work. With the coming of the Second World War all this was forgotten and it was only when I received a letter from Mum informing me that Uncle Dave had died that I recalled the fortune teller's tale. Aunt Dora moved to Sussex and it was some seven or eight years later that we heard she had remarried and how unhappy it had turned out. This did much to strengthen Mum's strong belief in gypsy power. When I was very small the sound of a bell on a Sunday afternoon sent me running out with a plate to the muffin man ... he rang a bell and carried the muffins covered with a white cloth on a tray on his head. We toasted the muffins at the end of a long fork in front of the fire on winter afternoons. Although the muffin man disappeared from the street early in the thirties, his memory was kept alive by a round-song that Dad made everyone join in at Christmas time. We sat in a circle with Dad standing in the middle and everyone had to sing a verse solo. Dad would sing to each of us in turn:

"Do you know the muffin man Do you know his name Do you know the muffin man Who lives in Blackwall Lane? "

and then each in turn had to sing in reply:

"Yes I know the muffin man Yes I know his name Yes I know the muffin man He lives in Blackwall Lane"

then everyone joined in the chorus:

"Yes she knows the muffin man Yes she knows his name Yes she knows the muffin man Who lives in Blackwall Lane"

and so on until everyone had been asked and the final chorus sung:

"We all know the muffin man" ...etc

Whenever Dad started this song I would sit in delicious fear waiting my turn and hoping I would not forget the words and let him down. When I'd sung my answer I would sit back with great relief and join in heartily with all the choruses.

For many years I believed that our muffin man did live in Blackwall Lane, which was only a few streets away from us, and it was some time before I realised that this was a song sung in other parts of London, obviously using a local street name.

Both Mum and Dad loved parties and we had plenty of singing at them. Mum had a lovely voice and could always bring a tear to the eye with 'Rose of No-Man's Land' and afterwards Dad would cheer everyone up with one or two music hall songs. He had two favourites, both of which had several verses with audience participation in the choruses. There must have been double meanings to many of the words because although they didn't sound funny to me the older men and women would roar with laughter and some of the younger people would go red and try not to smile as they took another sip of gin and lime. One song was called 'There's no toad in the toad-in-the-hole' and went on 'so give me a plate full of hole'. And the second one was 'Old King Cole'. I have heard some versions of the latter but none of them identical to Dad's. Most of the parties took place in our houses but other social events occured in local halls.

One was the Three Cups Hall in Earlswood Street which was a long hall with a kitchen that could be used for the making and serving of refreshments. This hall was used for Guide meetings ... Brownies ... Cubs and 'bun-fights' as we called the parties that these groups held once or twice a year.

Although I was never a Brownie or a Guide I managed to get in to one or two of these parties and Dad told me always to take a paper bag to bring back what I couldn't eat. I only went for the cakes and jellies because I thought the games they played silly and I never felt the urge to join one of the organisations. Fred had been a Boy Scout for a short while but I was too young to remember seeing him in uniform ... Later he told me he had left because he found it difficult to adapt what he learned to our way of life. I don't know if he was referring to being true to God and Country, or the do-good bit ... we as a small community did help each other out but this was automatic and there was never any religious message behind it.

CHAPTER NINETEEN

God played a small part in the life of the street, and with the exception of a Catholic family none of us went to church. We children investigated various denominations and sects at some time or other but nothing lasted long. The church at the bottom of the street had a small hall tucked beside it which was used for Mothers' Meetings and a society that was called the Young People's Union. A few of us went along every Wednesday evening to see slides of poor African children who apparently needed us to make them clothes.

To us theirs appeared a marvellous life, splashing about in wide rivers, living in perpetual sunshine, swinging large palm leaves to make a breeze. After the slides the Magic Lantern would be put back in the corner cupboard and we would stand and sing hymns before it was time to have a cup of cocoa or Bovril prior to prayers. Most of us went for the slides and the cocoa; the religious aspect becoming an occasion to snigger at the back and make jokes. We sang rude words to the hymns and when one of us realised that the initials of the society were YPU we would look at each other and ask as we sang 'Why pee you?' over and over again, until we collapsed with laughter and were sent out of the hall, eventually to be told never to return.

Our next religious kick took us to the Salvation Army hut near Maze Hill and here we lasted quite a few weeks on account of there being buns as well as cocoa for which it was worth behaving for half an hour or so. Further along the road towards Charlton were the Cecil Rooms, and these were let out for various functions and meetings. Some of the religious meetings were obviously of little-known sects for whenever we popped our heads round the door there would be only half a dozen people in the hall who chivvied us and shut the door firmly behind us, making it clear that children were not part of their religion. In any case we noticed that no refreshments were served so we gave up pretty early on.

The word went round that the new vicar at Christ Church was offering a free Sunday outing to all who attended his Sunday School for at least three months. I had never been to Sunday School although I was nearly ten at this time. I had no idea what was taught there apart from the fact it would be about Jesus, whose father had been a carpenter like mine, and as we had that story over and over again during our school lessons I couldn't see why Sunday Schools were necessary.

However the thought of a Sunday outing saw me enrolling the very next Sunday. We met in the same hall as the YPU and an elderly woman sat us in a circle on hard wooden seats before telling the same story of Jesus, Joseph and Mary that we already knew. Old Testament, New Testament, these meant nothing to me and as no-one bothered to explain them we just sat there week in and week out. I hardly bothered to listen to the monotonous voice droning on and on, but I was alert at the end when we filed out and were given a small coloured text.

These were rather beautiful and I wished I had kept mine but somehow after they had served their purpose I lost interest in them. Their purpose was all important as it was the saving up of twelve texts that showed you had attended Sunday School for three months. My texts were carefully stored in the chest containing my underclothes and I eagerly awaited the first Sunday School outing.

When we were told it was a trip to Bournemouth the excitement was almost too much to bear. None of the children had travelled so far. Dad was all against it. Bournemouth to him was foreign soil; what was wrong with Margate or Southend where he had his pub beano? However Mum said that Bournemouth was much nicer than Southend and it was the place that posh people went to when they retired.

The thought of the long char-a-banc ride was as much part of the adventure as the thought of actually seeing the sea. I took out some books from the library that showed pictures of Bournemouth and the beach with its large hotels. Mum was right ... it was posh.

At last the great day arrived and we were up early ready for the char-a-banc to set off from the church at seven-thirty. We would be back in Greenwich by nine-thirty in the evening and Mum said she would meet me off the coach. I had sandwiches and a banana for my dinner and sixpence with which to buy sweets. Dad told me to behave myself, gave me another sixpence as he thought there was bound to be roundabouts or Punch and Judy on the beach. Even Daisy and Fred who did not get up to see me off had left some money out for me the night before and I felt quite rich as I walked down the street to my waiting coach.

There was much noisy pushing and shoving as seats were exchanged so that best friends could sit together or in some cases a bully threw his weight about to sit at an already occupied window seat. Once more I was a loner as Marjorie was not coming on this outing. Having lived at the seaside for several years before coming to Greenwich it didn't have the same excitement or appeal to her as it did to those of us born in the street. My companion was a little boy of about four and soon after the journey had started he wanted to be with his sister and sat squeezed next to her in the seat behind. This meant the luxury of a whole seat to myself. The only form of travel I had known till then was a tram or bus, and the furthest I had been was through Blackwall Tunnel to visit Aunt Lil in her baker's shop in City Road. As shops and towns whirled past I was sure we would be in Bournemouth long before dinner time.

We stopped by the side of the road when we reached the countryside so that the vicar and Sunday School teacher could hand out lemonade, ice-cream soda, cola and bags of currant buns. After we had ate and drunk our fill we had ten minutes to run about and use the energy that had been stored up sitting in the coach. Before returning to the coach the vicar took the boys and the teacher escorted the girls to opposite sides of the road where we went behind the hedge to relieve ourselves. We could hear giggles and sniggers coming from the boys' side while we girls bit our lips and stared straight ahead. When we had finished we all waited for the teacher to 'go' but she marched us back to the coach leaving us wondering how she held it in.

Later the vicar stood up and suggested a sing-song and, starting off with 'Ten Green Bottles' and with the vicar conducting, we soon swung into a real party spirit. With us all concentrating on counting the bottles in the succession of verses none of us was looking out of the windows so it was a dreadful shock when we heard brakes squeal and the coach veered sideways to the crash of breaking glass. The vicar was thrown off his feet and confusion reigned as the screams and cries came from all directions. Eventually we were taken off the coach and lined up on the grass verge to be looked over for injuries. The coach was completely smashed in at the front and a small car was lying on its side in the middle of the road.

Miraculously no-one was seriously hurt; the vicar had a bruise on his face where he had hit the back of a seat in falling, two of the girls had cuts that needed a few stitches and the rest of us had minor cuts and bruises. Our driver survived with bruising and cuts while the lady driver of the car had suffered a fractured wrist and facial cuts. She had been overtaking us when a fly had gone into her eye and, temporarily blinded, she had veered into the side of the coach. Ambulances and a St John's First Aid team arrived and patched us up and as all our packed dinners were covered in broken glass they had to be confiscated and other food found for our mid-day meal.

We were on the edge of the New Forest, which to me looked similar to parts of Greenwich Park, and soon we forgot about the accident and were running about chasing ponies and picking wild flowers, while the poor vicar desperately tried to organise fresh transport. Our teacher started us off on some games and we thoroughly enjoyed ourselves, especially when the food arrived from families in a nearby village. The afternoon wore on and we were told we could not travel on to Bournemouth because there wasn't any transport available to take us and it was time to make arrangements to return home.

We waited while the vicar together with the local vicar and policemen huddled together to work out a plan, and to everyone's delight it was decided that we would catch a train to take us home. A local bus took us to Guildford and as this took a different route to our outward journey we found ourselves seeing new places - this was a really good day's outing, a train ride as well as a char-a-banc, another first as far as I was concerned.

I was surprised to see Dad as well as Mum, and when he saw my bruised face and bandaged arm he went straight to the vicar and started arguing while Mum hastily and indignantly took me home. However once inside I soon proved I was not hurt badly and I had enjoyed my day despite not seeing the sea - and then to my horror I started to cry. Mum said it was nerves and made me drink a cup of Bovril before going to bed.

I lay there watching Mum and Dad preparing for sleep and wondered how long it would take to save up enough money earned running errands to go to the seaside by myself. Dad broke into my thoughts; "Well, Blossom, that'll teach you a lesson, you only went to Sunday School so as to go on that bleedin' outing, didn't you? Told you no good'd come of it. Someone up there 'as got 'is eye on you my girl." I did not worry about ' 'im up there' - it was Dad's eye that frightened me much more.

CHAPTER TWENTY

Every September the street had a deserted air about it. Very few children would be seen playing in the street, there were few women at the street doors and to most school-teachers' horror, the new term started with a good third of the children absent. This was hop-picking time, and the children, mums and sometimes their dads went on an 'opping 'oliday. I longed for us to go with them but Mum was absolutely against any thought of it. Dad could not stay away from work because he didn't get paid to live in the country and pick hops. I could not understand why Mum wouldn't let me go because I could have accompanied any of the families from the street. But Dad said they lived like bleedin' pigs in sties, and he described a day's outing he had once taken which had included a visit to a hop field. He said they lived in huts that had one room only in which the families ate, washed and slept together. In fact most of the eating and washing and some of the cooking as well took place outside the huts. The only lighting was candles or oil lamps and cooking was over a wood fire. As for earning enough to repay a man's wages, most of it went straight into the local pub.

How I envied my friends when they arrived home with brown faces and arms telling wonderful stories of what they had done in the country. They had milk from the farmer which had come straight from the cow and when they came home they brought carrier bags full of large green apples. Mum was always given generous quantities of these by returning neighbours and I loved the juicy tangy flavour of the 'opping apples as we called them. To this day I don't know what variety they were. Throughout the next couple of months we had those apples stewed, baked or raw and our Gran, who was well known for being the best cook when it came to apple tarts, dumplings and pies, was kept busy baking for most of the Grove. She made her pastry in a large enamel bowl, cutting off the amount for that day's use. The rest was wrapped first in greaseproof paper and then in newspaper and was kept on the outside windowsill to keep cool overnight ready for the next day's ration to be cut off.

After Grandad died Gran spent more time with me during the summer holidays, particularly when she found time 'hanging on her hands'. Some mornings we shopped when she usually found a halfpenny to buy me something just for myself from Nobb's fruit stall - a large yellow banana or a pomegranate if they were in season. Over sweets I had no choice, she would allow me to buy only a bar of Nestles chocolate at Thomas's sweetshop near Blackwall Lane. This cost a penny which she said was good value and full of goodness. I always had to show her the red wrapper to prove I'd actually bought it no matter how much I preferred a liquorice stick or liquorice laces. "You don't know what's in 'em", she would say.

All her fruit was bought at Nobbs' stall on the corner of Earlswood Street, meat came from Parham's the butcher in Trafalgar Road and her vegetables from Lewis's in Tyler Street. I loved taking an empty bottle into Francis and Campion to be filled with vinegar. There were so many aromatic smells in this shop with its sawdust strewn floor for they sold paint, turps, ammonia, firewood in bundles and pine disinfectant. Another attraction was that we were given a halfpenny for every bundle of newspapers we brought to the man behind the counter. These had to be folded in half, untorn, and neatly bundled with string. The newspaper was used to wrap candles, firewood and small sales of nails, screws and tacks.

Next door was still part of Francis and Campion but here they sold groceries and bacon inside and on the pavement were displayed some dozen or more boxes of biscuits laid out on trestles. If we could afford it Gran bought half a pound of mixed creams to have with our morning tea.

On one memorable occasion, just before Easter, Gran bought me a small oval handbag, made of tin and painted in enamel with cream and pink flowers. Inside the bag were small round biscuits topped with tiny rosettes of icing sugar in different colours. I loved that handbag dearly, and it had pride of place on the mantlepiece in the bedroom, until it turned rusty and was thrown away.

One of the shops we always passed was Dales the piano shop, where sheet music was also sold and on Friday nights and Saturdays you could generally find a customer trying out one of the pianos, or someone playing the latest tune before buying the music. Gran never listened to music, as she was not interested, but as I grew older I found myself drawn into it and longed to be able to play the piano properly.

When we'd finished shopping and had a cup of tea I would find some excuse to go home as Mum said I was not to hang around Gran's at dinner time expecting a meal. I think she felt rather guilty at my being alone all day for six or seven weeks but there was nothing she could do about it. We needed her wages, she said, and I must put up with it. But of course Gran frequently did give me dinner on condition I did not tell Mum.

It was through being with Gran so much that I started to get interested in the cinema. We had three 'picture palaces' in Greenwich, the nearest being the Trafalgar, on the corner of Maze Hill near the Baths. My first memories of the Trafalgar was listening to the films from the outside. It was an ancient cinema and had only recently been converted to the talkies not long after I had been born. The local children quickly cottoned on to standing outside with their ears to the ventilator grids when you could hear, albeit muffled and echoing, the voices coming from the screen. And any afternoon during summer holidays you could walk down Maze Hill and see children pushing and scuffling to listen to the magic of the talking screen. We had no idea what the film was about, but it was enough to hear the booming voices and the sighs and laughter from the audience. The cinema attendant spent many weary moments chasing us away, but we were back as soon as he had taken up his position again outside the front entrance.

Grandad Nightingale did not believe in the talkies. Once they'd been installed he refused to go to the cinema again, claiming that it was all done by people speaking behind the screen. Not even when Fred, patiently explaining about recordings, could convince him otherwise.

This was brought back vividly when we saw the first moon landing. Dad was staying with us at the time and asked me to turn off the television as it was all trick photography. No-one could possibly reach the moon let alone walk on it. Nothing ever persuaded my father as with Grandfather Nightingale before him, that these things had actually happened. He mumbled and cursed over the newspapers for the remaining two years of his life whenever stories appeared of ever greater space exploits.

The other two cinemas were 'over the college' never past it, beyond it, or by it, always 'over the college' in West Greenwich.

A cinema stood at the junction of Creek Road and Greenwich High Road, Bluelights'. On wet afternoons Gran and I climbed up to the gods and sat on wide wooden benches that rose in steps from the brass railing of the balcony to the high domed ceiling. Our seats cost threepence for Gran and twopence for me in the afternoon weekdays but on Saturdays and Sundays they were dearer, costing sixpence and threepence. It was necessary to walk along and over the seats in certain places to reach the position preferred and there was always orange peel lying about - we always seemed to eat oranges at Bluelights', usually bought cheaply from nearby Greenwich Market.

Here I sat and watched Marie Dressler and Wallace Beery in the 'Tug-Boat Annie' films, and it was here also that I became envious of Shirley Temple. How lovely those short dresses were, how I longed for one ... and how quickly I saw other little girls in Greenwich Park wearing them. Soon Greenwich had a dancing school to teach tap-dancing. Red tap shoes were prominent in the shoe-shops and soon many girls were tapping up and down the pavements and we included this new skill in our street concerts.

I even managed to persuade Mum to let me have a few lessons; the Rainbow Babes Dance Troupe included me to put on a show at the Three Cups Hall when we tapped to 'Over my Shoulder Goes One Care' before it proved too expensive. But I kept my shoes and tapped up and down the street for many months afterwards.

The third cinema, another old building in Crooms Hill, had been used as a music hall when Dad was a young man. He recounted how they had had a cage at the back of the gallery and any rowdies in the audience were put into the cage for the rest of the show; he said they often got someone in the audience who became offensive to the entertainers. Not content with heckling and booing they would throw tomatoes and any other rubbish they had picked up in the Market. When things got too rough the management would, with the help of two large assistants, remove the offender to the cage where he could watch the show but do no harm.

But by the time I was about nine Barnards had been converted to a cinema and Tod Slaughter was all the rage. Gran became quite a fan of this early horror star, but as she was too scared to walk home alone afterwards she took me with her and so at an early age I too became a regular patron of Tod Slaughter's grim tales.

The 'Face at the Window' was particularly frightening, and so was 'Sweeny Todd' but the 'Ticket of Leave Man' I found rather sad in parts. These Tod Slaughter films were shown from about 4.30 in the afternoon so Gran would take a basin with her to Barnards and then on the way home we would stop at The Hole in the Wall, at the beginning of Trafalgar Road, to buy pease pudding and faggots for our supper. The little shop really was like a hole in the wall, with its low curved entrance cut into a stone wall; the shop itself was tiny, housing a low counter behind which stood pans of bubbling oil where fish and chips gently fried - along the far wall were large trays of pease pudding, saveloys and faggots. The back door stood open throughout the year to allow the smoke from the fryer to escape. The yard behind was just large enough to contain an old potato chipper. Fred had often earned sixpence or even as much as a shilling on some nights sitting at it peeling and chipping. Peeling was done by hand; when you had a bucketful of potatoes they were put singly into the chipper and shaped into thick, long chips, by pulling down a lever which lowered a square of cutting blades through the potato.

But to my disappointment Gran would not buy chips from any shops - they didn't change the oil frequently enough she claimed, and the stale oil permeated the chips - instead we bought a basinful of lovely golden squidgy pease pudding. There were also saveloys to be had giving off a tangy odour as their crimson glowing skins burst on biting, but again Gran wasn't happy about ready-cooked saveloys ... she preferred to get them from Parham's the butcher and cook them herself. But I loved the pease pudding anyway and as we walked home holding the hot basin to my tummy, Gran and I would discuss Tod Slaughter and I would relive that murky face rising through the mist outside the window and the woman inside the room turning slowly from the fireplace to see two searing eyes staring through the glass and my mind would echo her scream as she stood rooted with fear ... or else I'd hear that demonic laugh as the Barber's victim fell into the cellars below.

To the great delight of the local picture-going public we learned that a new cinema, a Granada, was to be built. It would be one of the most modern in the country, complete with organ. From that day on I was drawn like a magnet to the building site and along with hundreds of other children I impeded the workmen once free of school and home chores.

Gracie Fields was to open it and I determined to be at the front for my first live view of a film star. The manager promised us that after cutting the ribbon Miss Fields would sign autographs. The cinema was to be opened in the evening just after six o'clock and I hoped that Mum and Dad would finish tea quickly and accompany me.

When the great day arrived I rushed home from school and prepared a ham tea - as soon as I glimpsed Mum's scurrying figure - she always walked fast - I ran into the scullery, made the tea and quickly put the teapot down on the table near Mum's plate, popped on the cosy and impatiently waited for her to appear in the house. In my excitement I had forgotten to remove the bag that had contained the ham and as I put down the hot teapot on top of it I transferred the picture of the purple thistle onto our white tablecloth. I was sent to bed the moment Mum saw her ruined snowy tablecloth, and told to stay there until the morning. I didn't mind missing my meal but I pleaded to be allowed to see the opening of the Granada, but it was no use. Dad had now arrived home and he pushed me back up the stairs and made sure I was shut in the bedroom. I threw myself on the bed and sobbed ... I did so much want to see Gracie Fields.

After a while I tip-toed quietly into the front bedroom and I climbed onto a chair to look out of the window but all I could see were roof tops. Then suddenly soaring over them I heard Gracie start to sing 'Sally' ... the words were clear and pure and to my astonishment I felt tears pouring down my face. I stood alone on my chair, crying, laughing and clapping my hands, and when the song was over I crept back to my own room and felt that I hadn't missed the opening after all.

The next morning Gran told me all about it; she and Old Bill had joined the crowds outside the 'Granda' as she always called it. She had not gone in to see the picture because she thought I'd like a special treat and go with her on Saturday afternoon.

What wonders were revealed once inside the foyer that first Saturday; the decorated floor tiles, the carpets on the steps, the luxurious seats, those golden ornaments around the proscenium arch and what unbelievable lavatories!! The perfumed air cocooned us - and then I discovered that there was to be a children's Saturday club. I knew I could not afford to attend regularly but I did become a Granadier and loved to sing the club song, The Greenwich Granadiers, to the tune of the British Grenadiers.

This was the first regular entertainment specially for children that I had known. Other leisure activities seemed designed for adults with children watching from the sideline, pub-crawling, dog-racing, or even party-going; they were the only entertainments our family seemed to know, with one exception. That was the fair held on Blackheath. Dad and I went together every August, he wearing his Sunday best, watch-chain across waistcoat, hair parted down the middle, straw hat and bow-tie; really smart. The money for me to enjoy the fair was always found and I'd run across the Heath to clamber on the back of a large painted horse on the roundabout, one of three or four abreast, golden manes flowing behind, straight proud necks; and wicked looking eyes. Hot hands grasped twisted golden rails and tummies sank as the carousel started, the steam organ's cymbals clashing, drums banging, the horses trotted, cantered, galloped even faster, the fairground misty in the background. Then all too soon, it slowed and the ride was over. Sometimes though,without even asking, Dad would give the attendant the money for a second ride - the bliss of it all and the security of Dad's arms firmly round me as I walked giddily to the next treat; the chair-planes, or the swing-boats if I could find another child for a partner, as the boats needed two to pull on the red plush ropes and Dad alas would never ride with me.

Then it would be time for a plate of jellied eels for Dad and some pink candy-floss for me before we walked homewards down Crooms Hill, past the church where Mum and Dad were married. When she first met Dad Mum was in service to a doctor with two sons who lived in Crooms Hill, and it was from this very house that Mum was married, for the doctor knew what an unhappy home Mum came from and allowed her to be married from his own house.

We turned right at the bottom of the hill, along Nevada Street, where Dad stopped for a drink in the Gloucester; ice-cream and a glass of sarsparella from a stall outside the park gates in King William Street, for me.

On the pavement in front of the stall strutted hundreds of pigeons as in Trafalgar Square, where people were photographed with pigeons feeding from their hands or perched on heads or shoulders. Sometimes Dad would fancy having his drink in the Admiral Hardy, a pub inside Greenwich Market which was owned by a friend of his, an ex-Charlton Athletic football player, or maybe he would visit the Bunker, another pub near the market where I would have my usual tipple, a glass of grapefruit accompanied by an arrowroot biscuit.

After closing time we would walk home alongside the river, past the power station, the Trinity Almshouses and along Trafalgar Road and home to Mum, waiting with our dinner.

August Bank Holiday Monday morning - which he never forgot - was my time with Dad - for those few hours each year I drew close to him.

CHAPTER TWENTY ONE

One night after washing up the tea things Dad sat in his high-backed wooden armchair by the fireplace. Instead of reaching for his evening paper he sat gazing at the empty armchair on the other side of the fireplace. Mum was busy elsewhere with housework as she usually was in the evenings.

"Your Mum's going into hospital tomorrow", Dad told me. "You'll have to help keep things going here as best you can."

Hospital! The very word terrified me. My world was shattered. Something wrong with your Mum's stomach, was all Dad said - and even many years later, when I was a woman myself, Mum only said it was all to do with her working in the rope factory; the heavy work had damaged her stomach. But Dad, like other parents of that era, thought it unnecessary to inform a child of the exact situation so for the next two weeks my life was a misery as I could only foresee death awaiting Mum after her operation.

Then I realised how I would miss her - even though she was so rarely in the house when I needed her and even when at home she was always so busy that she had little time for me. But whatever happened during my day she would be with me at the end of it. Not a night had passed without my knowing that she was sleeping close by; now there was to be just Dad and me in four whole rooms and a scullery.

For Daisy was married and Fred, although still living with us, often spent the night with friends, using the house as somewhere only to keep his clothes.

Dad visited Mum every Sunday afternoon and one night during the week. The hospital was three streets away and I often found myself staring up at the rows of identical windows wondering which one hid Mum. I was not allowed to see her as children were not admitted as visitors, so I relied on Dad to tell me how she was. "She's getting on all right" or "She was pleased with your letter".. was all I usually drew from him in response to my urgent questioning.

I wrote to her twice a week but she never replied. And then, after a fortnight, Dad returned with a smile on his face. Mum had been allowed out of bed and could sit in a chair for a few hours each day ... she was almost well enough to come home. It would probably be another week before the doctors allowed her to walk up and down the ward, and if this went well she would be home a few days later.

I sang all Mum's songs as I dashed about the house, sweeping, polishing and dusting. Dad cleaned the bedroom windows because for this you had to sit on the windowsill outside, but I coped with the insides and the downstairs; using Mum's method of newspaper soaked in soapy water I made them sparkle a welcome for her.

On the morning Dad fetched her I whitened the doorstep with hearthstone and stood by the door to prevent cats or children stepping on it. Gran came to welcome Mum home and said Mum would be pleased with the house when she saw it. Dad had refused to let Gran help in any way with shopping, cooking or housework, with the exception of one Sunday dinner which we had had with her.

At last I saw Mum and Dad slowly turn the corner - she was holding Dad's arm as he helped her avoid tripping on the cobbles. She was white and strained as she sank gratefully into her own armchair while I made tea. Gran wondered why she had not been sent home in an ambulance, but Dad said it was unnecessary as we lived so close.

Although Mum had been warned not to work for at least two weeks she found it impossible to idle all day. Never one for books or needlework her life had allowed her precious little time to relax with these pleasures. Gradually she took over more and more of the usual household tasks but no matter how much she wanted to, she could no longer cope with the weekly wash. Since Mum's admission to hospital I had washed my own underclothes and Aunt Dora took over responsibility for Dad's best shirts, but the rest we had taken to the bag-wash. At first I was embarrassed carrying the white sack containing our dirty washing to the bag-wash office in the next street, and collecting it either later that day or next morning. But it soon became just another chore on the way to or from school.

Mum was never really happy with the result as sheets, tablecloths and clothes were washed together and not until we collected the bag was the washing released, still damp, for drying and ironing. A soapy smell percolated the clothes causing Mum to re-rinse handkerchiefs and pillowcases.

Laundering apart Mum was soon back to normal and within two months of entering hospital was back at work in the rope factory.

The doctors insisted that she be given work that did not involve pulling overhead ropes.

Her hospitalisation had been paid for by the weekly payments she made to the Hospital Savings Association, the HSA, that all working class people belonged to. The fear of being ill and not being able to afford treatment was a threat then that hung over every adult's head.

Of course Mum received no wages while in hospital, but she did get sick benefit because she paid a full contribution to the health insurance, her stamp at that time costing three halfpence a week.

Mum should have gone to a convalescent home, but this required extra payment by the patient and we could not afford it.

Until Mum's operation all our illnesses had been treated at home, by home-made methods. Every winter Mum made up bottles of cough and cold mixture to a recipe given her by Gran. I know it contained five ingredients including tincture of rhubarb, the only one I can remember. I would take a list to Barrons the chemist which they made up for me and bottled. Then Mum and Gran settled to boiling, mixing and stirring; the end product was a foul-tasting black liquid which was stored in old beer bottles or for that matter any other bottle, at the bottom of the food cupboard. At the hint of a cough or cold, everyone in the family was dosed. I remember one Christmas party when Dad brought out a bottle of Green Lady Cocktail, duly labelled and half a dozen lady guests were dosed with Gran's cough mixture.

I was the only member of the family who suffered from chronic sore throats every winter. My voice would disappear for days on end, and Dad called me 'rusty guts' for my pains - my throat was perpetually aching and very,very sore. I would be dosed with our cough mixture and sent to bed with one of Gran's woollen stockings wrapped round my throat; between the stocking and my throat were pieces of hot toast soaked in vinegar. With this unwieldly, wet soggy wrapping round my neck I was told to sleep and dared to move. Surprisingly enough I managed to sleep and obtained relief, but eventually I was taken to see the family doctor who had a surgery in Christchurch Street. Dr Silas was short, fat and bald with large myopic eyes behind his glasses. To my dismay and shock I heard him tell Mum that my tonsils should be cut out and quickly. So within weeks of Mum's operation I found myself in the same hospital. When I returned home a week or so later I still had a sore throat which I cherished annually into my late twenties.

When I was at Maze Hill School a smallpox scare caused us each to be given a notice to take home regarding vaccination. Although everyone in the family had been vaccinated for some reason unknown to me Mum had decided it wasn't for me. So now at the age of nine my teacher said if the forms were signed I could be duly jabbed at school next day. Dad passed the papers over to Mum who just shook her head and threw them into the fire.

This left me the only child in the class not vaccinated which made my teacher Mrs Waite so angry that she said she would come home with me after school and see Mum herself. I was terrified and told 'Miss' that Mum would not be home until after five o'clock but she was adamant and when school finished I found myself walking home alongside teacher. My face was burning with embarrassment ... you just did not do things like walking home with a teacher. As we walked up the street the women on the doorsteps followed us with their eyes and it was with a sigh of relief that I took my doorkey from my blazer pocket and let Miss into the house ... thankful too that I had washed up the breakfast things before going to school. Mrs Waite watched while I prepared tea and she asked me questions and seemed pleased to see me coping so well but I could see that she couldn't understand how a woman with a family could leave her household duties and work in a factory.

Lewisham, where Mrs Waite lived, was a slightly better area than Greenwich and I do not think she appreciated the depths of our poverty. Mum's scurrying feet sounded in the passage and as she came into the kitchen I saw her face reflect first surprise and then anger as she saw the teacher waiting for her. I was sent out of the house and as I sat on the window sill of our front parlour I could hear voices raised, coming from the kitchen, a most unusual occurrence in Mum's case.

After a short while Miss emerged, bade me goodbye and strode quickly down the street, avoiding the looks of the women on the doorsteps. Nothing more was said either at home or at school and I remained the only child in my class unvaccinated.

From then on however Mrs Waite seemed to try to protect me. She smiled at me whenever she spoke - if she was on playground duty she would walk over to the corner where I sat reading so rarely I joined in games at playtime. I invariably had a library book that proved too exciting to leave for long. On Friday afternoons her class was given a special treat. She brought to school a box of sweets which were handed out at the end of lessons - I always received extra, surreptitiously. I would be asked to put the chalk away, or get a duster and in doing so the extra sweet would be slipped into my hand. Neither of us said anything and this continued Friday after Friday until I left her class and sorrowfully made my way to Mr Martin and the top class.

Despite my lack of vaccination I caught no fevers but regularly I suffered chilblains every winter, in fact most of us in the house seemed to have them on our fingers and toes as our rooms were very cold, and there was no heating in the bedrooms at all. Gran had a standard treatment for chilblains which Mum forbade me to try but often I called on Gran only to find her with her feet in the po, soaking her chilblains in the urine she had passed during the night ... she swore by this and said it did more good than the creams and lotions we bought at Barrons and Milners, the two neighbourhood chemists.

But when a wart appeared on one of my fingers Mum let Old Bill 'talk' it away, but not before we had tried a painful and ineffectual proprietary brand guaranteed to burn it off. So I went to Gran's where Old Bill held my hand, gently stroked the wart and murmured to himself. He was simply asking it to go away ... and it did just that a week later. I should have been surprised I suppose, but I wasn't, and neither was anyone else.

The sight of an ambulance with its dark blue windows sent us children off screaming as we ran "touch your collar, never swallow, never catch the fever." If we managed to say it before the ambulance disappeared from sight then we believed we stood a good chance of not catching the particular fever that patient was suffering from. Of course, if we saw the ambulance while out walking with our parents, we held our collars and muttered to ourselves as quickly as we could before the ambulance went round the corner and many a Mum or Dad had looked down in amazement at their offspring to see a hand grasping the coat collar tightly, lips moving in silent prayer.

Shortly after I left hospital another member of our family was admitted ... this time it was Fred.

He had recently bought a new bicycle with three speed gears. His front wheel caught in the tram lines throwing him off when he was hit by a van, fracturing a shoulder and breaking a leg. He was out of work for several weeks, hopping about with one leg in plaster. Dad's comment was that it served him right for going in for modern contraptions, but Mum in fact felt relieved. Bad luck she believed came in threes so now that a third member of the family had been in and out of hospital safely she could stop worrying. If only she had known what was in store her fears would have only just begun.

CHAPTER TWENTY TWO

With enforced time on his hands Fred found time to think and eventually faced Dad to tell him he was giving up his apprenticeship in the barge-yard. He no longer wanted to be a barge-builder or to have anything to do with the river. He had decided to seek work in the Siemens factory, a large electrical and telephone factory in Charlton that employed several thousands of people.

This brought the house down about our ears. Dad went berserk and the arguments between Dad and Fred became almost violent. Mum and I would leave the kitchen as they shouted at each other, banging the table, knocking over furniture. If things grew too rough then we went next door to Aunt Dora's and sat there over a soothing cup of tea until we heard the front door crash indicating that either Dad had gone to the pub or Fred to his friends.

It was the beginning of a rift between father and son that finally separated them shortly after Fred married, Fred not visiting Dad once during a two-year illness and not even knowing when Dad finally died, a bitter frustrated old man.

To Dad's way of thinking a factory-hand was like a caged animal. It was all right for women he said, more natural for them to work indoors, but not for men. He told me I would find it easy when I obtained a factory job on leaving school. There was nothing else worth doing for a girl, he claimed . . . plenty of money and women to talk to all day. He would sit in his chair after tea, unread newspaper in hand and call me his Blossom, telling me not to be led astray as Fred had been and that it was wrong to get above my station in life.

I'd listen, wanting desperately to tell him that I hated the thought of factory work. I didn't know why as I had never seen the inside of one but I listened to Mum and Daisy talk, and Mum's rope factory especially sounded horrific ... imagine so much noise around you that you could not hear anyone speak !

Marjorie and I often talked about what we would do when we grew up ... it was good to have someone who understood me. She too had no plans for a career when she left school but in her case there wasn't the same compulsion to work; her parents looked upon education as important and Marjorie knew that whatever her father planned it would be for her benefit.

One thing we agreed, and that was to take ballroom lessons and learn to dance so that we could go to the weekly dances at the Town Hall, or the Baths. Dancing was very popular and on Saturday evenings we saw young women with long dresses walking along the road with their boy friends and we longed to dress like them. This was one of our dreams ... far removed from factories.

Fred eventually secured a job at Siemens and so, aged eighteen, after four years' apprenticeship as a barge-builder, he started off another long period of training, which this time he completed and became a qualified electrical engineer.

Once his evening school studies started he gave up much of his drinking and betting and often stayed at home with me, the pair of us poring over books on the kitchen table.

His love of greyhound racing however continued and most Saturday nights found him at a dog track in preference to a dance hall, where most of the lads went to show off to the girls. They wore smart new suits, shiny shoes and slicked down their hair like Ronald Colman.

No sooner had the household settled down to accepting Fred's new way of life than I jolted them. I found a job.

It was for Saturday mornings only but I felt inordinately proud. There were few girls who worked on Saturday in the thirties, apart from paper and milk rounds which were for boys, few girls could find odd jobs.

It all came about one afternoon on my way home from school when I saw Molly, the cook, standing at the pub's side door, who beckoned me - Molly, a tiny quiet Scots woman, was rarely seen except in the early morning when she rushed along the pavements shopping. She never appeared behind the bar, her job being simply to cook for the landlord, his wife and the other living-in staff, and prepare cheese or ham rolls for the bars but nothing else. Pubs were places for drinking in not eating.

Five lived in; the landlord, his wife, Molly, a barmaid and a barman-cum-cellerman. Extra staff were hired at weekends; the potman a pensioner who collected the glasses, and Nellie,who cleaned the bars and did the rough in the rest of the pub. And now I was being asked if I would like to help Molly every Saturday morning from eight o'clock to midday. I said yes straight away without stopping to think about wages ... but Molly insisted I get Mum and Dad's permission and to tell them I would receive a shilling a week. I didn't know if Molly had help before and if so what had happened to them. I didn't care. I was going to earn some money of my own.

For the first time the cobbles slipped easily beneath my feet as I rushed home exploding with my news. Mum was pleased and said she was sure Dad would let me take the job on and of course he didn't hesitate believing we were all work fodder and anyway the Crown was his local. He told everyone in the pub that night that his girl was working for the missus now.

Look after yourself he told me, do as I was bid and I'd be all right. Pub jobs were good ones, maybe I would find myself settled already when I left school.

Pub instead of factory? That was an idea I hadn't considered before.

When Saturday morning came Mum woke me before she went to work and gave me a white apron neatly ironed and folded. She said she expected I'd need it; when she had been in service the cook always appreciated girls having their own aprons, even when they were provided with a uniform. It indicated they were expecting to work hard.

My excitement vanished, to be replaced by fear as I approached the pub ... what would they want of me? I had been running errands for people ever since I could remember a whole sentence ... fingers tightly clutching a sixpence or shilling while I repeated "a quarter of tea please ... quarter of tea please ... quarter of tea please" but to work in a pub kitchen, now that was something quite different .

The missus, as the landlord's wife was known, was set apart from the other women who used the pub or lived in the street. She served occasionally but only in the Saloon, and she would also talk now and then to one or two special customers in the Private, but never, ever did she condescend to help in the Public Bar.

Her glamorous dresses, shoes and hair style matched those in the magazines ... and when I discovered that she regularly had her nails manicured I knew she must be very rich. A manicure became my yard-stick for wealth ... who else would pay to have their nails cut?

I had seen her only when opening the bar door to ask for a drink or return my empty glass ... a queen-like head and shoulders behind the bar wreathed in cigarette smoke who sometimes gave me a nod of that elegant head, and a smile.

Molly opened the door to my timid knock and I followed her into the kitchen. I stood nervously by the side of a dresser, looking around the largest room apart from school classrooms that I had ever been in. The table was scrubbed white like Gran's and the floor was quarry-tiles in black and white squares. A large coconut mat stood just inside the door and a black, red and yellow rag rug in front of the big black kitchen range. There were two large white sinks with wooden draining boards on either side of them and a second dresser entirely covered the end wall. On its shelves were a dinner service in willow pattern like Aunt Dora's with soup tureens, vegetable dishes and large and small gravy jugs of whose purpose I was then entirely ignorant. In the drawers were tablecloths, tea towels, cutlery, kitchen knives, sieves and old newspapers, neatly folded which were used to cover the tiled floor, immediately after scrubbing, until it dried.

There was also a gas stove, almost twice the size of Mum's. In that kitchen I was to learn the rudiments of running a house, and I look back now and wonder if it was also there where I developed my first love for cooking and catering that played such a large part later in life. It was a homely kitchen, one that was to become familiar and friendly always with Molly there to listen to, learn from and to talk to. But the work was hard and that first morning my shoulders ached after carrying vegetables from the street corner stalls. Potatoes were bought in twenty-five pound sacks and as it was impossible for me to carry that amount I walked backwards and forwards with ten or twelve pounds at a time. Apart from potatoes I fetched the potherbs, carrots, turnips, onions, swedes and fruit as well.

Nothing was delivered. Either Molly herself or I would buy it and it had to be good, ripe, firm and no bruising.

Most of the stallholders knew me but once I had started working for the pub how different their treatment; no longer was I passed off with old squashed tomatoes or limp lettuce. The pub was held in esteem by most of the town, especially the trades people. Anything not quite up to standard and Molly would be round to tell them off, her strong Glasgow accent coming to the fore, even though she had lived in London for many years.

Steve the barman and I would get the worst of Molly's tongue too if we walked over her newly scrubbed floor before she had put down her newspapers, words lashing out over us as if in a foreign tongue. When she was riled I simply failed to understand her. But she soon forgave us with the help of an old earthenware teapot from which she would dispense sweet tea accompanied by scones, hot and crumbly straight from the oven.

Sometimes Molly would recount stories of her own childhood in Glasgow where she lived in a street very much like ours. When she first came to the pub the neighbourhood had made her feel homesick. I told her that I had never felt like that and that I had made up my mind to quit the area as soon as I could and never return.

It was wrong she said to be ashamed of one's background. I couldn't change where I had been born no matter what I did in the future, and she reminded me that my parents were forever part of me however much I rebelled against their way of life.

I can hear her now, as I write the words, and I know that it was due to Molly more than anyone else that I grew to understand my parents and their attitude to life, even though so different from my own.

On the first Saturday morning I went to the shops, paid the bills, helped make the rolls for the bar and then swept the long passage-way from the door, past the kitchen and out into the yard. Molly inspected my work and was satisfied that I had lifted rather than merely swept round the rubber mats.

In the kitchen a glass of grapefruit and two ham rolls waited for me. As I steadily ate my way through these she laid sixpence on the table before me and remarked that she had decided to put the other sixpence in the Post Office every week for me so that I would not waste my money.

There was no question of asking if I agreed to this; she had decided and that was that. As it happened I had already decided that I would save part of my wages so that I could pay for music lessons.

As the weeks passed my shopping speeded up and I began to spend more time helping Molly in the kitchen. It was with her that I learned how to make soups, pies, scones, cakes and I had had no idea you could make jam at home ! When it came to ironing Mum had taught me well and Molly was delighted when I skilfully ironed some of Steve's shirts. She would never let me press the guvnor's however or carry the elevenses into their private rooms. I could prepare the tray, smooth the tray cloth, put out the cups, saucers, spoons, sugar and milk and a plate of biscuits, but Molly had to make the tea in a small flowered teapot, fill a jug with hot water, straighten her apron, smooth her hair and on the first note of the church clock striking the half hour at 10.30 take it upstairs to their first floor living room.

It was four months before I saw the inside of the missus's living room, or to be exact, her parlour where she interviewed me. Until then I had to put up with Molly's short sharp answers to my many questions as to what the missus was really like. Were her rooms posh? "Aye, they're grand" ... "too many fol-de-rols" ... "Madam's one for comfort."

But Nellie, the daily who came to do the rough, loved to chat. Nellie almost crooned over the curtains in the parlour, "real plush velvet me love, that's what they are ... plush and lined. Coo I wouldn't mind 'aving a bit of that linin' meself for me front room" ... "I shine 'er mirrors up so's even me looks good in 'em", she would grin, and then seriously "shouldn't 'ave all that silver Hornaments lyin' around though. One of these days someone's comin' right through those bleedin' back windows and take the lot, stands to reason, knowing them that lives round 'ere - still mind you that room looks lovely, like a bleedin' palace."

I was allowed to wander anywhere downstairs in the pub but forbidden to go upstairs, the staircase was the preserve of those who lived in.

At first I found it exciting to open the door almost opposite the kitchen and find myself in the Saloon Bar which was not patronised by Mum and Dad and so was unexplored territory. With the Crown almost to myself as it were, I would walk down the two steps into the Saloon, sit in one of the easy chairs and look at the pictures; Swiss mountains with ultra blue skies and cotton wool clouds high above miniature boats on a blue lake. I loved the feel of the deep wall-to-wall carpet, the first I had seen. We made do with lino and mats at home.

A long wooden settee leather seated stood on one side of the room in front of which stood a table topped with a brass rail.

Several smaller tables and groups of chairs seemed to kneel before the bar, gleaming in the sunlight shining through the top half of a vast engraved window.

A partition of oak panelling with glass along the top divided the Saloon from Dad's bar, the Private, which was small and narrow, two benches along each side and three small tables in front of each bench. The bar had a rolled top, to the side of which stood a glass barrel containing arrowroot biscuits. Lino graced the floor of the Private.

Next came the Public Bar, the largest of the three, forming a corner and side of the whole pub. Here the floor was of a black composite material, much like the asphalt surface of our school playground. Wooden benches flanked oblong tables along the walls, while a scatter of chairs grouped round smaller tables. This was the busiest of all the bars and from opening to closing time there was always someone here - dart players, punters picking winners (the Crown was convenient as an unofficial bookie lived in our street) or maybe someone waiting for a cribbage partner. A thick cloud of smoke permanently hung midway between floor and ceiling in the Public. Most of the men, Dad included, rolled their own cigarettes; only the younger men bought ready-mades. A few of the really old men still clung to their clay pipes and the smell of tobacco was ever present even after Nellie or Steve had scrubbed the floor with Lysol.

Getting to know Nellie was something that helped me over a childhood fear, for Nellie lived in Orlop Street, one of the more notorious neighbourhoods less than five minutes' walk from our street but one I had not dared visit. It was an alley that ran parallel to Trafalgar Road, the haunt of witches who could be seen puffing away at pipes which Dad said contained dried used tea-leaves. Indeed we even had such an old woman in our own street. But the Orlop Street harridans terrified us as did the alley children. But in getting to know Nellie I realised that they were much like ourselves, but they in fact were the real poor, those people who lived in Orlop Street.

To me Nellie was an old woman although she could not have been more than thirty-five. She had five children and her husband was out of work more days than he was in. Nellie said he couldn't find the right sort of job to interest him, for which she uttered no blame, instead she and her mother undertook regular cleaning jobs leaving him sometimes still in bed when they went out each morning. Nellie had no fault to find with her life. "Mind you, we could always do with a bit more", she would say, "still we're all the same in our street and no-one'll alter it."

When I told her of my dream of leaving the street to discover what the rest of the world was like, she was horrified. She thought it quite wrong even to contemplate leaving my family. She could no more think of living away from her Mum than she could of flying, and saw nothing wrong in marriage to a drinking out-of-work layabout. That was what her Mum had suffered and she expected no more for herself.

One day when I was wandering through the empty bars I saw Nellie take a small square medicine bottle from beneath her apron and half fill it with gin. The bottle was returned to some spacious pocket under the apron so quickly that I knew this was a regular occurrence. As she turned back to her bucket and broom she saw me, and a grin spread across her face and she winked, "They don't miss it, love, and I only takes it on weekends as a treat for me Mum".

I wasn't particularly shocked, after all most of the children in the street shop-lifted and when Woolworths had first opened most of them no longer bought sweets, they were laid out in such enticing rows on such easy counters that in no time at all even the very young became adept at slipping a chocolate bar up their sleeve. But I decided that Steve the barman should know, for he was responsible for the stock-taking. I approached the subject carefully asking if he knew exactly what he had behind the bar. Misinterpreting he thought I was interested in helping him and so asked Molly if I could, whenever I finished the shopping early.

And so the following Saturday I found myself helping with the bar and cellar stock-taking. It soon became apparent that my mental arithmetic was at least as good as Steve's, although he had been doing it for several years, so helping Steve became a regular Saturday job as well.

I still worried over the gin that Nellie was taking and eventually told Steve. To my surprise he roared with laughter. "Of course I know she takes it, and a bottle of Brown Ale for herself. The missus knows as well, but don't you go telling Nellie, or she'll up and leave and we won't get as good as her for a long time."

And that's how I learned that in the pub trade all take pickings, not too much, as Steve said, but just a little now and then. Most landlords realised that it was part of the trade. "Why", he went on, "I shouldn't be surprised if you didn't help your Mum out with a bit of something now and then." A quick denial came to my lips to be smothered even as the thought shamefully came to me that Molly occasionally gave me a few slices of ham, or a lump of cheese to take home.

I had accepted gratefully, thinking they were hers to give but now I appreciated they were no more hers to give than the gin was Nellie's. Understanding my dilemma Steve said, "Now don't worry and don't refuse Molly when she gives it to you or you'll only upset her and we know what she's like when she's upset don't we?"

And so I continued to take home my perks for which Mum was always grateful and Dad would nod and smile saying I had my head screwed on the right way, getting myself fixed up in a pub so quickly.

The pub certainly influenced my life. The other children, watching me stagger back with loads of vegetables, would shout and jeer, "Stuck up ... going all posh ... think yourself everyone cos you work in a pub." Up to then I had not realised that the pub was admired in our community as a meeting place for men, as a loan club, a savings club, and of course where they arranged the one day by the seaside each year.

But it was my weekly shilling that interested me most. I even managed to save some of my half each week.

From my sixpence I would buy comics and sweets but the rest was put in a jug on the dresser alongside the other jugs into which every Friday Mum put the rent money, coal money, insurance money. Two shillings was also put into a cracked flower vase for emergency use. New shoes for me counted as emergency.

Soon I would be able to start music lessons. I had found a place near Vanburgh Hill where I could have them for sixpence an hour but first I had to save enough money to buy a manuscript book and music book. I knew that Molly would give me the balance of my earnings at Christmas and so decided to have my first lesson in January.

I had just finished the shopping one Saturday and was about to help Steve when Molly said that the missus wanted to see me in her parlour immediately. I felt excitement, fear and shock ... what on earth did she want to see me for? I had been working almost four months now and had seen her as she went up or down stairs when she had only nodded to me. I asked why she wanted to see me but Molly had her straight face on and bade me to go to the lavatory, wash my hands and smooth my hair. Then she pulled my skirt neat and gave me a push towards the stairs. "Go on, she won't eat you!" I walked slowly up to Madam's sanctuary. In answer to my knock a voice told me to enter, and with a shock I realised that the deep, posh voice I had imagined sounded far fruitier with more than a hint of Cockney telling me to "Come in."

My feet sank into a carpet far more luxurious than that in the Saloon, and as I followed the beckoning beringed finger, I looked about me at Aladdin's cave.

Everything sparkled and shone. There were mirrors on three of the walls, two of which reflected floor to ceiling views of the opposite walls. As if hypnotised I was in an everlasting tunnel of mirrors, doors with rooms leading to rooms with mirrors, leading to doors with rooms ...

My eyes took in silver ornaments on small tables, silver framed photographs on the marble mantlepiece, a big clock in a gilt frame. Mantlepieces usually had a mantle-cover made of chenille with bobbles or a fringe, but this was coverless; the marble gleamed reflecting silver above. The fender was of brass, as was the coal scuttle and small brush and shovel. A pair of black velvet mittens lay by the side of the scuttle so that no coal dust begrimed hands when laying or replenishing the fire.

I stood in front of one of the two velvet settees and looked at my employer for what was really the first time. The air around was heavy and odorous with perfume and she sat so erect and still that she looked like a wax-work figure. Her hair in stiff symmetrical waves seemed glued to her head; her raspberry lips were drawn in the fashionable bow of Daisy's film star magazines.

She smiled, revealing large and obvious false teeth, as she asked if I liked working in the kitchen with Molly. I nodded, my voice having deserted me. She went on to say that she knew Mum and Dad and it was hearing Mum talk about how well I was getting on at school that had made her think of me as a help to Molly.

I couldn't believe my ears. Mum actually talking about me? The missus continued asking questions and then she said that her son and his wife were coming to live in the pub shortly and that later they would probably take over the business.

More help on a permanent basis would be required and if I did well as a Saturday girl then there would be a good chance of staying with Molly as full time help.

Here was my chance to escape factory work, but deep down inside I rejected a career as a kitchen maid, much as I liked Molly.

Seeing my hesitation she smiled and said there was plenty of time to decide as I had two years or more before leaving school, but she liked to plan well ahead.

Meanwhile, she continued, she would rather I took on another little job instead of helping Steve, and she pointed to a brown velvet cushion on the floor beside her. There reclined a very fat pekinese, apparently fast asleep, until I bent to stroke him whereupon his little eyes shot up in the creases of fat and hair and his tongue slobbered as he growled.

The missus told me not to be frightened of her naughty Chong, as she tapped him lightly on the head saying he was a naughty Chongy-Wongy. And she fed him a chocolate.

The extra job was to walk Chong after the shopping. He was lazy, she said, and had insufficient exercise. It would do him the world of good if I took him for a walk once a week.

From then on the worst part of my Saturday job was my half hour with Chong. I'd rather have carried a whole sack of potatoes or done the stock-taking on my own than try to exercise that lazy creature.

He flatly refused to walk. I'd put him on the ground, and place a chocolate in front to get him started. This he would eat promptly, sit down again and refuse to budge. I'd pull and tug and he'd be content to slide on his pads until I worried that I was hurting him, when I would pick him up and carry him to the Park. Once on the grass I would try again, but it was no good; even if I let him off the lead and threw a ball he would gaze at me as if I were daft. When other dogs bounded after his ball he would merely look at them with narrowed eyes but make no move at all.

Thoroughly spoiled he lived a life of far greater luxury than any child in the street. Why, his consumption of chocolate creams cost more than we spent on meat and fruit. I felt no compunction whatsoever in eating half his chocolates.

I did feel guilty however when I returned him to the parlour and his mistress would cuddle him and tell him to "say thank you for your lovely walk Chongy, what a lucky boy you are", popping another chocolate between his fat slovenly lips. She claimed she could see how much better he looked and she knew how much he loved me now; he no longer growled when I picked him up. I suppose he had got used to me, but as for loving me (or me him) that was wildly out.

But as Mum often said "It's an ill wind" ... and from the tribulations of Chong's walks I found a Sunday morning dog-walking job with Aunt Dora's wire-haired terrier, Kim. And what a difference. Kim loved to run, bark, play with a ball, roll down the hills with me. Before breakfast on Sundays we would spend a good hour roaming the park and it was the most enjoyable threepence I had ever earned.

In the summer the landlord and his wife went to Switzerland for their holidays from where, to my delight, she sent me a card showing the place they were staying in. Dad promptly took the card down to the pub that night to show his mates how well in his girl was.

And I had a bigger surprise when they returned home and gave me a present of a bracelet, made of square wooden links with roses painted on each link. It was the most beautiful thing I had ever possessed and I found every excuse to wear it. Again Dad was as pleased as if he'd received it himself.

I hadn't told him about the offer of a full-time employment but I wondered if anything had been said to him by the missus or even Steve. As I grew to know the missus better I felt she was on my side. She often lent me books although she never asked me about them or whether I enjoyed the stories. I feel she had read few of them herself, but there were a great deal of books in the room next to the parlour and I read my first Dickens and Daphne du Maurier from the pub books. She enjoyed music though and I often heard Mendelssohn's 'Fingals Cave' on her gramophone.

And so the year passed. Soon Christmas drew near and one Saturday Molly told me to cut Chong's walk to a quarter of an hour only as she wanted to see me in her room before I went home. It was paying out time for the rest of my wages.

I knew Molly well enough by now to know that she would not merely hand the money over. I would get a little talk and some advice as well. She was always telling me not to worry about what people said, "Get as much education as you can while at school and don't stop afterwards, you must keep learning all your life." As I made my way up to the little room at the back of the first floor landing I knew that I was in for another little lecture but I didn't mind as I was going to see inside Molly's room for the first time.

It was as neat and tidy as Molly and contained a wooden bed with matching dressing table, wardrobe and chest of drawers. A small table stood by the window and a chair with a cross-stitch cushion and on the mantlepiece stood photos of the family, in wooden frames and a china ornament which read 'A Present from Margate'. This had been bought for her by Steve when he went on the pub beano.

Molly brought out a Post Office Savings Book and solemnly handed it over to me. "There's a sixpenny stamp in there for every week you've worked." I thanked her and then there was a silence. Finally Molly said "Now then, don't waste it, you've worked hard for that, so you should think hard before you spend it." I told her that I already knew what I was going to spend it on.

Music lessons!

She was puzzled and I think annoyed ... what on earth did I want to do that for? I told her I wanted to learn to play like Billy Mayerl or Carrol Gibbons, but she didn't know what I was talking about and thought I was throwing my money away, didn't I realise that it took years and years to become a musician? Even as she spoke I knew that one of the reasons for my obsession was really that I didn't like not knowing what all the dots and circles meant on the music. I knew that what Mum played was wrong and resented my inability to show her what was right.

This need to know was like a disease, driving me if I read something I couldn't understand to elicit the answer from a teacher, the library assistant or perhaps Marjorie who being a year older knew more. And now, eleven years old I knew it was music that I wanted to learn, this was my immediate need; I had to be a dance band pianist.

CHAPTER TWENTY THREE

Like all children, Christmas excited me and I hoped that the longed-for present would appear at the bottom of my bed. Over the years I had received dolls, black and white, a doll's pram, a doll's house, my stocking inevitably filled with a tangerine accompanied by puzzles, a sugar mouse and crayoning books. Christmas Eve was one night when I was not left alone; Mum and Dad took me with them to the pub; to The Queen, the William IV, the Brick and finally of course to the Crown.

After the pubs closed we usually had half a dozen or so friends come back to our house for supper while I would go to bed. Usually I had fallen asleep on the steps of the last pub or two but I would be sleepy enough to drift away even as Mum started to play the piano.

Dad insisted on filling my stocking and placing my present at the foot of the bed himself, but he made so much noise dropping the tangerine which rolled beneath the bed and of course cursing, while on hands and knees he retrieved it. The larger present would be banged on each successive stair as he humped it up the narrow dark staircase to prop it against the bottom of the bed. I knew from a very early age the truth about Father Christmas but I didn't dare tell Mum or Dad. Once the gifts were on the bed that was as far as my own Christmas went; from then on it was a time for adults, for drinking, eating and party-going. Each year I wished that we could have a Christmas Tree, but although Daisy and Fred always made paper-chains and even bought paper bells from Woolworths which we hung in the passage and front room, my first Christmas Tree was the one I bought for my own children.

We had mistletoe though, a piece hung from the gas bracket in the passage and everyone, including me, was kissed heartily whenever guests arrived.

Christmas dinner was always roast chicken, sprouts and roast potatoes, sometimes followed by Christmas pudding but not invariably.

We had plenty of apples, oranges and nuts in the front room bowls. I loved Christmas afternoon when Mum and Dad went upstairs to rest and I could sit beside the specially lit front parlour fire and eagerly read my new annuals which I received from Gran, Daisy and Fred. My dolls, pram, doll's houses, as they arrived each year were quickly forgotten. They were the kind of toys that needed the company of other children to make up games with and as Mum did not like me to invite children into the house and she said the pram would get broken if I played with it in the street, well of course it soon became obvious that these gifts turned into a liability. I was constantly being reminded of how much they had cost and how ungrateful I was not to play with them. I would have preferred presents that I could use in the street, like hoops, skipping ropes or a scooter. One year it seemed that all the children were playing with diabolos;

how I longed to balance it on the rope and throw it high in the air and catch it again ... but Christmas meant a big present, that Mum and Dad thought suitable even if unusable.

However, I did get my scooter. Fred made me one out of an apple box. Once he had put on the wheels and secured the handle-bar I was away like the wind. I didn't mind that it was unpainted.

Boxing Day was the day that I had to take my big present round to show Gran, Aunt Dora and anyone else in the street Mum thought ought to see it, and then Gran came back to dinner with us.

Everyone went to work the next day and soon Christmas was tucked away and often forgotten until I would see my new black-faced doll, lying dusty in her pram and I'd remember how much I had wanted a pair of skates instead.

Photographs supplied by:
Halstow Road School
Greenwich Local History Library
Iris Bryce

Trafalgar Road
Greenwich Baths is on the right

Greenwich Gas Works, Tunnel Avenue

Entrance to Blackwall Tunnel

Above: Horse team, Trafalgar Road
Bottom left: Trafalgar Road, Blagrove florist's and Greenwich Ignite Supply Co.
Bottom right: outside lavatory, back yard Woodland Street where the author was born

Corbett's Boat Yard, Crane Street
The 'Rafts', a local name, were for hire

Above: Barge Yard, Charlton in the 1940s

Left: Angerstein Wharf

Left: Church of St. Alfege from end of King William Street

Bottom left: High Bridge 1927

Bottom: Greenwich High Road. The workshop for blind is just off left

Left: Grocer's in Church Street

Right: Church Street,
'Bluelights' cinema is just off left

Charlton Athletic Cup Final 1947

Above: Sam Bartram, Charlton Athletic's renowned goalkeeper

Top left: Woodland Walk (previously Woodland Street)
The author lived second from top

Right: Chapel of Trinity Hospital

Junction of Church Street and Greenwich High Road

CHAPTER TWENTY FOUR

The time approached for me to leave junior school and start at Halstow Road Elementary School. The school stood at the top of a steep hill leading from the main Woolwich Road, a mile away. When I knew that Marjorie would be coming with me I didn't feel so bad.

Before leaving Maze Hill, the top class was taken on a day's outing to Lullingstone Castle, near Eynsford in Kent, twenty miles away, to see some Roman remains and the silk worms that Lady Hart Dyke kept and bred there. We sped through Eltham, Sidcup and Swanley, gradually seeing more green fields and as we swooped down Farningham Hill the white chalk downs appeared in sight.

In Eynsford we paddled in the ford fed from the River Darent where we ate our sandwiches and drank ginger beer.

At the Castle we were introduced to Lady Hart Dyke, a real Lady, who had probably met the King ... and she was actually talking to us about the life of silk worms. We were shown the trays of wriggling worms and watched them eat an enormous amount of mulberry leaves. Daringly I showed off telling Lady Hart Dyke that a mulberry tree grew in Greenwich, which she said was unusual.

Next day in the playground Keith Barton opened a matchbox to show me a silk worm stolen from the Castle, he wanted to know where the mulberry tree was that I had mentioned as it hadn't eaten any of the Virginia Creeper leaves that were lying in the box. After school we went down to the river and along the towpath towards Trinity Hospital, a home for some twenty pensioners in whose garden the ancient mulberry tree stood.

Nicking things and avoiding authority were second nature to Keith and in no time at all he was back over the wall with the mulberry leaves stuffed in his shirt. We ran back along the towpath and once in the narrow Crane Street we carefully opened the matchbox and fed small pieces of mulberry leaf to the worm and to our delight he started munching.

We got fresh supplies daily but after about a week our worm died and we buried him in the mud near the Trinity Hospital Wall.

CHAPTER TWENTY FIVE

At last the day came when I enrolled at Halstow Road School and what a chaotic, muddling but unexpectedly happy day it was.

First Mum had surprised me by buying the new uniform the school liked their pupils to wear which was not compulsory. So dressed in my new navy blue gym slip with school badge, snow white blouse, navy reefer coat and matching velour hat complete with blue and orange band, I started off, the proud owner of a new brown leather satchel, a present from Fred.

Marjorie and I joined up along Trafalgar Road and chatted excitedly about the unknown future. The school building was similar to Maze Hill School, but far larger and it was many days before we learned our way around.

Mrs Belbin was our Headmistress, a plump elderly lady with a gentle face, hair neatly coiled into a bun at the back. She told us the school rules and of the opportunities offered. She made a special point about homework; only illness could excuse at least one hour's work at night.

To my delight Marjorie and I were in the same class; our teacher, Miss Bell, had a pretty smiling face and I took to her immediately. Our classroom was on the top floor where I was seated four tiers back from the teacher's desk and from which I could see the Thames - many hours were to be spent watching the ships and cranes instead of working at art and needlework, at which I was hopeless.

From that day onwards my satchel was always stuffed with books; I loved walking along feeling it swing against my back. And the very first week of my new school life I visited Nellie's house in Orlop Street to tell her excitedly of my new life. It was almost certainly because of this visit that tragedy struck.

The school nurse, known to us all as Nitty Nora, inspected the new entrants. One by one we were called into the room used for medical examinations where she looked through our hair to see if we were infected with lice or nits. To my dismay and shame they were found on me and I was given a letter to take home which prescribed the necessary treatment. My name was added to the pile of yellow cards denoting that I was now included with the unclean.

Mum's first reaction was to scream with horror. I was sent down to Baron's the chemist for a steel-toothed comb as used by the nurse, Lysol and an antiseptic shampoo. Armed with these Mum washed, rubbed, scrubbed and combed unmercifully through my short thick straight hair which contained a multitude of nits. Night after night Mum combed them on to newspaper which was burned on the kitchen fire. I endured a month of this painful treatment until she was satisfied. Miss Bell was as upset as I and assured me that it was just bad luck. Mum's treatment was successful but throughout the rest of my schooldays at Halstow

Road that yellow card, a mark of disgrace, followed me from class to class. I never again felt entirely free and happy, always waiting for the day Nitty Nora came and a monitor would come into the classroom bearing the yellow cards and I would have to step down from my desk to join the 'specials'.

CHAPTER TWENTY SIX

The newspaper carried constant stories of the coming war with Germany, as did the radio. But I was thirteen years old and my world revolved round school, playing in the street and reading in the public library. Even the gas-masks with which we had been issued now lay in the bottom of the cupboard, forgotten.

Then came the day when we assembled in the school hall after dinner. The headmistress, her staff ranged round her on the dais told us that the Government had ordered the evacuation of children from the big cities; war was likely to be declared accompanied by bombing, especially of factory and dockland areas like ours.

Our teachers had the necessary forms explaining everything to our parents, and these were to be signed and returned the following day. Our destination was not then known, but in due course we would write home and no doubt our parents would be welcome to visit us.

There was more, much more, but I stopped listening to her after realising that here at last was my chance to quit the street. There was no fear in my mind that it might be just as poor and wretched, I knew it wouldn't be, and in any case if our teachers were coming with us it was sure to be a really nice house. I imagined us all living like my Angela Brazil schoolgirls, and I couldn't wait to snatch up my forms and rush home with them. Not once did I worry about leaving Mum and Dad, getting shot of the street was all that filled my mind.

As we sat over tea Dad and Fred talked about the war. The forms were still in my satchel as I knew that Mum would only put them behind the clock until the meal was over. Before tea was finished Daisy arrived and told us that Charlie was going to enlist in the Army, and Fred said he would be going too. Mum went very white and Dad told her not to be stupid; did she think he was going to rush off and join up. No bloody fear, he'd done his bit last time and he had no intention of doing any more.

Daisy produced a leaflet which had been tucked under our door knocker, and when Dad read it he gave a grunt saying that the bloody Government was wasting its money again; workmen would be erecting an Anderson air-raid shelter in our back yard on Monday.

Things were happening fast ... I decided it was time to reveal my news, but before I could do so Aunt Dora and Uncle Dave came in from next door to discuss the air-raid shelters.

I was sent to buy some beer and when I returned I gave the jug to Dad along with my evacuation notice. He sat up abruptly and with a roar shouted for silence, "Listen to this, evacuation of children ... " He then read out the notice. Aunt Dora who had no children of school age put her arm around my shoulders and nodded while Mum sat silent. Dad finished and looked at me.

"You're not being bloody evacuated. I'm not letting anyone take my child away from me. You belong here, at home with us." No-one spoke and I felt tears spring to my eyes and I blurted, "but Mrs Belbin says ... "

"Sod Mrs Belbin, you're staying with your Mum and me."

The rest of the evening was a nightmare as I listened to the horrifying talk of bombs, food rationing and poison gas, all apparently imminent.

Next morning I had to tell Mrs Belbin that my evacuation papers had been torn up and burned. Obviously my father had been upset she said and hadn't meant to throw them away, but I explained that he had no intention of letting me leave. At this she was extremely cross and said I was to tell my father that she would be along to see him at eight o'clock that evening. I was terrified and didn't know how to tell Dad, but it had to be done. I couldn't have her just walking in and catching him unawares. Goodness knows what would have happened. So I told him that I had got into trouble because he had thrown away the papers, that I was the only girl in my class not going, and maybe the only one in the school; and that the headmistress was so worried about my safety that she thought it a good idea to explain the evacuation to him and Mum personally and she was coming tonight. He said he'd be waiting.

When she arrived I was sent out of the house and it wasn't very long before I saw Mrs Belbin leave, her face very white and tears glistening in her eyes.

At the end of the week the headmistress told me the school was closing and that the children were being evacuated in two days time. Emergency schools would open in a month or so for those children who were left behind and in the meantime I could keep any school books I required for I must try to keep up my studies as best I could. Miss Bell would advise me before she left.

CHAPTER TWENTY SEVEN

At Maze Hill station I felt driven to watch my classmates board the trains. A jumble of children, parents, goodbyes, tears, smiles, laughs ended abruptly as the last train drew out. The station cleared of tearful Mums returning to empty homes while I went back to a childless street.

The next few weeks were more lonely and bitter than I would have thought possible. Even Marjorie had gone - not with the school but privately with her Mother and all the children with the exception of the oldest brother who was now working in the shop.

I rarely spoke to Dad - the little affection I had for him had now been drowned by his selfishness.

When I heard that a school was opening in Blackheath Hill for two days a week I immediately enrolled not even bothering to tell them at home. I was on my own now, simply waiting to grow up and get out. Within a couple of months some children had returned home from Hastings, where most Greenwich children had been evacuated, as they missed their parents so much, but the majority stayed and for the first four months of the war I was the only child in our street.

On joining the school at Blackheath Hill to my dismay I found that the other children, some twenty in all, were under the age of seven and I found myself helping the little ones, giving rather than receiving instruction.

And so my formal education ended at the age of thirteen and a half. I never forgave Dad.

After a far from merry Christmas Daisy brought an application form for employment at the Siemens factory where she worked. If I would take it along on my fourteenth birthday, a few weeks off, she was certain a job would be mine.

I took the form but said nothing, as I had my own ideas, none of which unfortunately came to fruition. Up and down Trafalgar Road I marched asking shopkeepers if they wanted assistants but not one offered work. So I was forced to go to the pub and see about being Molly's full time help. But the war had changed the missus's plans and her son was no longer living with them. The Saturday job was mine as long as I liked but full time, alas no.

Then dear old Miss Hussy, who kept the little sweetshop in Earlswood Street, told me that a woman in Charlton employed three girls on knitting machines in the basement of her house to make shawls and baby clothes and now there was a vacancy. I set off immediately to walk the two miles to the house in Charlton which was a large one half way up Church Lane.

I was taken downstairs to a big room containing three knitting machines, two large and one small. Two girls were busy at the larger machines, throwing shuttles with wool through threads stretched on wire frames, chatting to each other and nodding and smiling to me. It looked so simple and the atmosphere was easy and pleasant. I could start on the morning of my fourteenth birthday.

My news was not received with pleasure at home but I ignored their reaction ... I was the one to make the decisions from now on about my future.

I duly presented myself for work at eight o'clock on a cold February morning in 1940 and to my horror found that by ten o'clock I had failed to master the machine. The wool was in a tangled mess round my feet ... in and out of the chair legs, hopelessly knotted in the machine itself ... and much worse, the pay was by piece-work, so much for each shawl, so much for each matinee jacket, which made me realise that this kind of work would never be for me. I did not produce two good rows of knitting in the next three hours. I went home at dinner time and did not return.

Not wanting to admit failure I told them nothing at home but realised I had to do something before Friday as Mum naturally would expect a wage packet to be handed to her.

Every Friday after the tea things were cleared away Fred and Daisy gave Mum what they thought a fair share towards the house-keeping. As a newcomer to the world of work I would be expected to give Mum the whole of my wage-packet and she would give me what she decided would be enough spending money. Dad of course never surrendered his wages; Mum received thirty shillings a week from him throughout the thirties to cover food, rent, insurances, the lot. The rest he spent, he never saved a penny.

The next morning I called at the Youth Employment Office and was given an insurance card and registered for work. Factory work only was available they said, giving me a green card and instructing me to report to a place in South Street which had been a shop and looked even smaller. About fifteen girls sat at benches and on a dais at the end of the room was a glass-partitioned office where I was interviewed by a young Jew, very smartly dressed with Brylcreemed hair. His gold teeth gleaming he questioned me about my school, education and then said I could start immediately. Wages ten shillings a week.

We inserted spirals into lipstick cases so that, when the cases were filled, a twist at the bottom of the tube caused the lipstick to emerge. The day passed picking up spirals from a box on my right, inserting them into tubes from a box in front and depositing the finished container in another box to my left.

That evening I told Mum where I was working. She could not believe I had changed jobs within forty-eight hours ... no-one behaved like that. It was bad enough when Fred gave up the barge-yard after four years, but to leave after one day I would end up a bad lot if I went on like this, that I was lucky enough to find another job and I was to make sure I stuck to it.

So there I was, if not a real factory, at least in a job that was equally boring. I wondered how long I could stand it, but once again the situation resolved itself.

After a fortnight the boss asked me if I would like to work with him in the office, as he thought I was different from the other girls. He often needed extra help with the paper work and that he would teach me. We were in his office, away from the benches, and coming over to my chair he put one hand on my shoulder and with the other he smoothed down my hair, which I wore straight with a deep fringe, unable to afford a perm favoured by most young girls. He went on to say that there would be more pay and that I need not start work so early.

Something told me to get up and run, but I needed the job badly ... and the money. He sensed my fears I suppose, because he smiled and told me to go back to the bench and think it over.

When it was time to go home one or two of the girls sniggered and asked if I was going straight home or did the boss want me for overtime.

I knew then that I couldn't stay ... and after tea that night I took the only way out.

I called on Daisy in her flat near Westcombe Hill and said that I'd like to work in Siemens.

Within two weeks I was one of the many thousands rushing to clock in and out, fighting for a place in the tram queue, morning and night. The hours were 7.45am to 5.30pm Monday to Friday and 8am to midday on Saturday. Wages were twelve shillings and sixpence a week. So I had already achieved a rise of half-a-crown but what was important was Siemen's encouraged their staff to study and I was allowed to finish work at 4. 30pm twice a week to attend evening classes. Thus deviously did I discover a pinhole of daylight at the end of my long tunnel.

CHAPTER TWENTY EIGHT

He put his hand on my shoulder and looked down into my eyes, "So you're my new red light girl."
I could not answer being breathless after climbing all those stairs to this room, high up on the fourth floor. It was filled with young girls, older girls and even older women. Their ages ranged from fourteen to sixty and they were to be my associates for most of my days from now on. This was the dreadful moment that had clouded my life for the past year or so - my first day as a factory worker. I was now one of the mass of factory-fodder, soon to be conditioned by the alarm clock in the morning, followed by the starting hooter, and then an interminable gap of boredom before the final hooter released us all, all seventeen thousand of us, from this factory alone, bursting like peas from a gigantic pod.
On this, my first day, I had hoped that Daisy would arrange to meet me on the way to work, but I was left to battle through the pushing throng of bodies all trying to board the first tram that came along. I found myself tightly jammed against the other standing passengers, handbag tucked beneath one arm and dinner-time sandwiches which were in a brown paper bag, becoming damp and crumbling as I clutched them in desperation from sliding through sweating fingers.
The fare from Greenwich was a twopenny workman's return and I suffered in silence whilst the energetic conductor elbowing and clicking his way down the tram grinned at me querying my age, "Who's the bleedin' workman then darling?" I was used to this ridicule. I knew I was undersized and still had not started to use lipstick and powder so therefore looked more like a schoolgirl than a working one. I stood as straight as I could and repeated my request for a ticket and at last was given it, accompanied by a pat on the head and smiles from the men and women standing around me.
At Westcombe Hill there was quite a change-over of passengers as this was the beginning of the factory area stretching along the road through Charlton and into Woolwich. From the outside the factories, huge brick buildings with hundreds of lights glowing through their windows, all looked alike. To all my questions Daisy had merely replied, "Your foreman or charge-hand will tell you all about it."
As I left the tram I saw Daisy with two other women, all walking very fast. I ran to catch up with them. "Hello", I said. "Thought I might have seen you on the tram." She continued her hurrying.
"Go through Middle Gate, not this one or you'll never find your way back to Personnel and they won't like it if you are late on your first morning." And she followed the rest of the moving throng through Gate No 1 ... leaving me to turn around and run back to the main road and along to Middle Gate.
The factory made telephone equipment, cables, batteries and electronic equipment ... all important war work. The area covered by the various buildings was vast and there were three tram stops between Gates

1 and 3, and the buildings stretched back as far as the eye could see, to the edge of the river.

I remembered Personnel from my interview and here I was met by another girl about my age. "Your name Iris?" she said. I nodded. "Follow me", she replied and turning round she left the room at a run. I remembered Daisy's hurried footsteps and the rest of the workers as they pushed and jostled to be the first off the tram, and now this girl running ahead of me . . . was this another part of the system? Never walk when you can run ... hurry hurry hurry your machine awaits you.

We ran down the road passing large brick buildings of four or five storeys and although it was only eight o'clock in the morning I noticed that through these windows too many rooms had their lights on ... hundreds and hundreds of electric light bulbs, some with green enamel shades, others bare and gently swinging.

We walked to the end of this road and at the last building my guide stopped. "Here you are, fourth floor, Mr Anderson. Oh, this is 'L' Building and that gate there is the best way for you to come in. Get off the tram at Warspite Road. It saves that walk from Middle Gate. Bye."

She ran off whilst I tried to get some breath back before climbing to the fourth floor of 'L' Building.

On the ground floor just inside the door was a clock ticking away the minutes, edged on both sides with racks and racks of brown cards, all named and numbered. Further along the wall were double doors, I gently pushed them open and immediately the noise that met me was deafening. I saw nothing but vast machines, with belts flying around metal wheels, water gushing from narrow spouts over pieces of metal being drilled ... no not water, but a milky looking liquid ... the noise and smell of oil made me close the doors quietly, but of course no-one noticed me and I ran up the stairs to the first floor. Here the glass panes in the door were painted white and although I stopped and listened through the crack I could hear no sounds at all coming from this room. I ran on up the wide stone stairs to the second floor where I saw what looked like hundreds of women sitting at long benches, no-one saw me looking through the crack, they were all sitting with heads bent, intent on their work on the benches.

I suddenly realised that everyone was working, I WAS LATE! I tore up the rest of the flight, past the third floor and breathlessly came at last to the fourth floor. I pushed open the door and a chattering of voices, sounding like a lot of birds in an aviary, rose up and floated around me.

A man in a brown overall was just inside the door, it was Mr Anderson, waiting for me - his new red light girl.

The room stretched the length of the building and down the centre, almost side by side, were two very long benches. Girls and women sat facing each other across them and the constant flow of their chatter and laughter intermingled with the soft hum of machinery and the clanging of metal as screwdrivers,

99

spanners and drills were used and discarded, apparently without any of their operators even bothering to look either to see where they lie on the bench or where they were replaced. Hands stretched out, fingers grasped, pressed, turned, twisted, all without a glance. Eyes were firmly fixed on the object in front of each operator.

I was handed over to a girl who told me she was the other red light girl and she showed me where the cloakroom was and found me an overall which hung almost to my ankles. I was taken to stand at the end of one of the benches.

It was then that I noticed that running down the centre of both of the benches was a moving black rubber belt. A woman stood on a couple of steps at the beginning of the belt, raising her high enough to be able to see right down it and I watched fascinated as she placed different articles on to it at certain intervals. This part of the factory made telephone equipment and our floor put together the many components that finished up as head-sets, breast-plates and mouthpieces.

My job was to keep the workers supplied with the screws, nuts, washers, bolts, webbing and a hundred other things needed to complete the article. When an operator saw that she was getting low on anything she put her hand up and switched on a red light bulb that swung above her head. I then ran to her, took her order and went to the far side of the room where the stores were situated. Pushing the small rectangular tin containers underneath the grille I'd shout for 13BA screws, hexagon nuts, felt washers, and a box of insets and all the time I had to keep my eye out for the next light. The belt must not stop - I must not keep anyone waiting - I soon joined in like everyone else and swore at the poor storekeeper if he kept me waiting too long. That part came easy with my street upbringing ... "Quick with those bloody nuts, I've three more soddin' lights on ... What's the matter with your bleedin' ears mate, 3 BA not 2" . . . and so on and so on, running down to the next light, hoping that she had not let herself get too low, "Christ, another light, I'll never manage it" ... Always run, run, run.

But I did manage it and what I thought was impossible took only a fortnight to achieve. My legs and feet still ached at the end of the day but it was bearable and forgotten after a while. To my astonishment I even found time between runs to watch the 'feeder' whose job struck me as the most fascinating in the room. The complete operation from feeder to where the pieces of equipment tumbled into crates, not only completed but inspected and packed - all this had been timed by Them - The Time and Motion Men. Sometimes one of them would sit by the side of a girl, stop-watch in hand timing the fixing of a piece of webbing to a breast-plate. If she was quicker than had been previously timed a different interval would be worked out for the feeder who would have to place webbing and bakelite breast-plates on at a faster rate. This of course meant re-arranging the rest of the belt which upset many of the women but made no difference to the timing now instituted. But the feeder did seem to have just that little bit of independence denied the rest of the women and I noticed that each one liked to work out her own method of marking up the belt.

Nora, who looked after my belt, marked her time intervals with coloured cardboard strips. These hung on overhead wire - when a mouthpiece reached the yellow marker it was time to put on another, the webbing was fed on at a green one, more earphones at the blue, another breastplate at the brown, the large insets at the white, whoops! that webbing is already at the green, and yes - another mouthpiece, an inset, more head sets. Nora stood surrounded by large crates of these components, Queen of the Belt, her eyes never strayed as she automatically stretched down, across or even backwards, her fingers obediently clutching the correct object every time.

As I watched Nora ambition stirred in me ... I would like to become a feeder, to feel the power of controlling that belt and its output of work. To see down at the end of the room the completed equipment, inspected, packed and stored by the lift, and know that you had helped to achieve it. I told Nora this, but wise woman that she was she just smiled and said, "You have helped as well ... we're all dependent on one another here." And at the end of my first two weeks I felt proud to see all those crates by the lift ... I was really one of the workers now.

My life now consisted of two separate worlds. There was the Monday to Friday world when I woke up and immediately began to go through a series of actions keeping to a strict routine. This included my morning wash in the kitchen, after everyone else and after Mum had made a pot of tea, then followed the ritual slice of bread and butter and cup of tea for breakfast. I was the last to leave so I washed up the breakfast things, leaving them ready for tea time.

Then I grabbed my sandwiches for dinner, which had been made up the night before, and it was time to run down the street and join the regulars at the tram stop at Blackwall Lane - all of us hoping to get on the first one that came along. Some fifteen minutes later I would be running down Warspite Road, Woolwich, through the gates and fighting for my card to clock in. Then scurrying up the stone stairs with the other hundreds of women, to get changed into my overall just in time as the hum of the motor warned that the belt was starting.

The morning tea-break was bliss ... when the belt actually stopped for ten minutes. Then it started again until dinner time. The afternoons seemed to fly past with only aching feet to remind me of the hours which were already history.

And then a repeat of the mad morning scramble for the tram, and at last home. After tea I usually read or sometimes spent the evening with Marjorie.

That was my Monday to Friday world with the added excitement of wages being paid on Friday afternoon. Mr Anderson handed our packets from his little glass-partitioned office that stood by the side of the stores. I received 12/6d per week, less my insurance stamp and I felt very proud when after tea that first Friday I handed it over, unopened of course to Mum. In return she gave me back my fare money and half-a-crown.

The second world was one in which at first I took very little part. This was the week-end world, where dancing, going to the pictures or football, or dog-racing or drinking were paramount. All talk or thoughts of the factory world were banished completely, this was a time to dress up, go out and spend your money. It was not long before I soon found that both these worlds had swallowed me into their systems, pushed and pummelled, re-shaped my whole outlook and spewed me out, and in such a short time too ... I was at last another unknown cog in the vast industrial wheel ... and I liked it!

CHAPTER TWENTY NINE

Getting up early was never a problem to me or any of the family, we were all conditioned to it. I would lie in my small bed, tucked into the alcove alongside Mum and Dad's big bed, and watch Mum dress, she knew I was awake but she never spoke until she was going downstairs. "Come on now, get up, and give your brother a shout", and without waiting for any results she would continue down into the kitchen. After the kettle was filled and the gas heard to plop alight beneath it, Dad would start to grunt a bit as he now raised himself up in bed and started to dress. His shirt hung over the bottom rail and he would stretch down the bed and tug it off, then pull it over his head whilst still sitting up in bed. He would then get out of bed, put on his trousers and socks and if in a good mood come over and rumple my hair before he too went downstairs to join Mum in the kitchen. Dad's working clothes were still the traditional style that had been worn by generations of barge-builders. A buttoned up shirt in a thick heavy material, no tie of course. He wore this winter and summer, the only exception being that on cold winter days he wore a 'choker' tucked inside the neck of the shirt. His jacket and trousers seldom matched as they were leftovers from his Sunday best suits, patched and darned. On arrival at the yard the jacket was removed and a pair of navy blue dungarees put on. He always wore a cap and the peak would have been pressed into the right degree of curve over the years.

Hats were an important demarcation of status in the yard, the foreman wore a bowler hat, and all the manual workers peak caps. In the thirties many of the young office clerks wore trilby hats, the latest fashions in these being copied from the American films, but some of the older office managers still wore a top hat.

When I heard Mum filling the kettle a second time I knew that the tea had been made and the rest of the water poured into the enamel bowl waiting for Dad to come down and wash. I always shared the second kettle with my brother Fred, Mum having washed from the first kettle.

We all hastily swallowed our cups of tea, grabbed our dinner sandwiches and one by one left the house. Dad first, he started work at seven o'clock, then Mum left a few minutes later and Fred usually went at the same time as he now travelled to work by bike because he was saving up to get married and the weekly fare was religiously put aside with the rest of his savings.

I left last, having washed up the breakfast things and set the table ready for tea. I started work at a quarter to eight, when the streets were aired, said Dad, telling me how lucky I was to have such a cushy job.

As the weeks became months I became more and more firmly drawn into my two ways of life. At work I met and spoke only to those people around me, inside the four walls of L Building, fourth floor. I had settled down much easier than I had thought, my nightmares of factory life were receding and I had had no more rebellious thoughts such had tormented the last two years of my life. I was happy - or thought I was, until the day I noticed a sunbeam again.

Standing behind Nora, watching her feed the conveyor belt I suddenly saw a sunbeam slanting through the window and onto the belt. My eyes followed the dancing, swirling, dusty shaft down onto the moving black shiny surface. It looked like a river now, flowing gently along, the bakelite pieces of telephone equipment placed on it were tiny boats, sailing down the river and out to sea, and then on and on to ... Shouts and shrieks from the bench made me look up, and there swinging like flaming swords in the air were FOUR RED LIGHTS!

I ran up and down, grabbing tins, boxes, switching off the glowing bulbs, rushing over to the stores ... run, run, run.

By now I could easily memorise five or six operators' needs at a time, balancing the small oblong tins on my wrists and arms, sometimes carrying two or three on top of each other.

I had learned that being small had its advantages. I could run fast, nip in front of others at the stores counter, use my elbows and swear back as good as them.

But that sunbeam, like a golden dart, had pierced the protective shell that, unknown to myself, I had put around me in order to survive my new world. It was as if I had been living in a vacuum - I seemed to wake up and on looking around I immediately sank back into self-pity. After all I had said, promised myself, vowed, proclaimed my protestations to the family, here I was working in a factory and apparently not bothering about any ambitions, ideals or dreams. I wasn't even as good as Dad, he at least had a trade, he was a craftsman, but what was I? Just a faceless number shut up in this building day in day out. Why I was worse off than a worker-bee, they did at least know who their queen was. But who was Mr Siemen? Was there one, or was it just a made-up name? And what did I mean to him ... just a brown clock-card - if that.

I wondered if any of my colleagues ever felt like me? I tried talking to Nora about the way I felt but she only said, "It's the weather love, soon as Spring's here we all get funny feelings. Take some sulphur tablets, ever so good for you, they cool the blood."

I gave up, if Nora didn't understand me then I knew the rest of them wouldn't. They hardly spoke to me during tea breaks, I was too young to be included in their incessant chatter about boy-friends, fiances or husbands and as most of them were usually knitting furiously whilst talking and drinking tea, and as I had still not mastered the art of reading a knitting pattern, then I was well and truly outside the pale. I wondered if their fingers had become so automatically used to moving when working on the belt that they just had to give them something to do during break times; the intricate Fair-Isle jumpers and gloves were swiftly fashioned even as I admiringly watched.

The other red light girl was a year older than me but she looked much older, she was well established with the girls on her bench and she eagerly looked forward to being promoted to attain their status and sit by their side, switching on her red light for the runner.

I could not help it, I felt that sunbeam inside me, telling me that it was Spring outside and I longed to breath some of the cool fresh air instead of the stuffy warmth of my factory cocoon.

I started to have my break time sitting on the landing outside the shop door. The stone steps were cool and I could see the tops of some trees through the landing windows, their branches showing bright fresh green leaves unfurling - pointing straight at me, telling me to come out and see them.

That night, after tea I walked through Greenwich Park, my sanctuary, and the one place that I realised I had ignored for the past few months. My feet found their own way to that extra special place. I did not notice if there were children on the swings or old ladies walking their dogs, I saw nothing until I was on top of my hill, looking out far and wide. I relaxed and let my eyes wander over the roof tops of riverside palaces, rows of little grey houses, tall factory buildings, swinging derricks from the docks and finally they rested on something glinting in the evening sunshine ... a tiny golden cross on top of a huge dome far away in the smudge of London smoke.

Once again the old magic was there, in front of me ... my tension slipped into easy relaxing dreamy waves, pouring over me. I could breathe again. This feeling frightened me at times, made me wonder why I was so dissatisfied with my given way of life ... why was I so restless? I also knew too that I was lucky to have been given just a tiny piece of ambition to explore and discover what life was meant to be.

CHAPTER THIRTY

During the early months of 1940 the highlight of my week was the ritual visit on Saturday afternoons to Greenwich Baths with Marjorie. Now that I was a working girl I could afford romantic smelling bath cubes and talcum powder and I bought these on my way home from work on Saturday morning, usually in Woolworths, where they were laid out in a vast tempting array and one could lean over the counter smelling lavender, sweet jasmine, rose, or exotic sandalwood, until the senses reeled under the pungent aroma being energetically sniffed.

After a hasty dinner usually of spam sandwiches and a cup of tea, I would collect a clean soft towel from the ottoman which stood at the foot of Mum's bed. This would be carefully rolled round my soap, bath cube, flannel and tin of talcum powder.

Greenwich Baths were only a few minutes walk away, along Trafalgar Road and after buying our threepenny Slipper Bath ticket I would feel the excitement mounting as the hot steamy water cascaded into the deep enamel bath. The only bath known to me until now had been the tin one in front of the kitchen fire every Friday night, and although this sounds warm and cosy, in reality it was an uncomfortable cramped affair, made even more awkward by bending and crouching in order to avoid the draughts of cold air coming at you on one side from the ill fitting kitchen door, and from the badly hung sash cord window at your back. Movement was limited in order to avoid spilling the water over Mum's rag rug. So no wonder I eagerly watched gallons of water pouring into a gleaming, if somewhat scratched, enamel bath, knowing that it was all for me, in my own private cubicle.

I could lie back wallowing in my new found luxury, not caring if my hair got wet as it hung straight down anyway, but Marjorie and most of the other girls tied their hair up in turbans, or in some cases the well-off ones wore waterproof shower caps. If I shut my eyes then it was even better, for the Municipal Baths disappeared and in their place was that fabulous bathroom belonging to a famous Hollywood film star. Photos of the star and the bathroom were to be seen in many film magazines, and now as I breathed in deeply of the scented air around me I knew exactly where the white fur rug was on which I would step out, draping the huge white sheet of a towel around my glowing soft body, then seated at the enormous dressing table, that had mirrors at the back and the sides, perfumes and powders would be chosen from a vast array of bottles and jars.

But this dream never lasted long, there was too much noise all around me. Eyes open again I would lay and listen to snatches of conversation as girls called out to their friends in the next cubicle, their voices echoing up and down the tiles and marble gangways.

Marjorie did most of the talking between us at this time in our friendship. We were still real, true friends, but she was already in a slightly different world to me. She worked as a book-keeper in a laundry at Blackheath Hill. Her wages were not an essential part of the family budget and although she gave her mother a token payment she could spend a great deal each week on herself. She was always dressed in the latest fashion and went to ballroom dancing lessons and to the weekly Town Hall dances. She was, to me, a real grown-up person, whilst I looked and felt no different from the schoolgirl of a few months back.

But for a short while on Saturday afternoons I became her equal, at least in my dreams. As Marjorie called out over the partition telling me what she would be wearing for the dance that night I would see myself in the dress she described, it would be me twisting and twirling in the arms of a tall dark handsome partner. "Why don't you come with us tonight?"

I opened my eyes, my shoulders immediately feeling cool as they emerged from the hot water.

"Why don't you?" It was Marjorie's voice again.

"What do you mean?"

"Why not come with me to the dance tonight, it's only a small one at Charlton, you'll enjoy it." Marjorie yelled louder over the splashings and the taps gushing out more steamy water, the slamming of doors, the gurgle of water running out of a dozen baths, and the giggles of girls as they wrapped up wet towels, flannels and soap and clicked their high heels down the echoing rooms.

Until this moment my Saturday nights were usually spent at the pub with Mum and Dad and so it was with mixed up feelings of excitement and fear of the unknown that I found myself, after tea, standing in front of the square tip-up mirror on the dressing table in my brother's bedroom.

And I didn't like what I saw - a small girl with short straight brown hair, cut in a thick heavy fringe. She wore a black pleated linen skirt and a white blouse, the latter had been a left-over from schooldays; over the top of the blouse was a fair-isle sleeveless pullover. But as my gaze travelled downwards and I tipped the mirror over a bit more I felt better, for my legs and feet looked glamorous in real silk stockings and my first pair of high-heeled shoes. They were brown suede court shoes with two-inch heels.

I thought the bottom half of me looked more grown-up than the top half, but there was nothing I could do to alter my outfit. I did have however one real piece of feminity to add. On my way home from the baths I had gone into Woolworths again and after much deliberation I recklessly handed over sixpence for a small bottle of California Poppy perfume. And this I now liberally dabbed on to ears, neck, wrists, hair and for a 'make sure' super effect, a final shake or two over the front of my pullover. I felt great now and I laughed at the girl in the mirror and flew down the steep stairs, my new shoes and feet as one, and grabbed my coat off the nails Dad had banged into the passage wall. A yelled goodbye to them in the kitchen and a glow of satisfaction as I banged the street door behind me. It was Saturday night and I was going out leaving them behind in the house.

I eagerly listened to Marjorie's chatter as we rode in the bus up Westcombe Hill and then walked along the Charlton Road to the small hall standing by the side of Our Lady of Grace Catholic Church. She told me that tonight's dance was run by a local promoter; he usually put one on every month and always had a good band which attracted super dancers, some of whom she already knew.

I felt a bit nervous as I followed her across the hall and watched a man throwing handfuls of chalk over the floor.

"French chalk, makes it easy, especially in a slow foxtrot, this floor gets awful sometimes."

I had no idea really what she meant, but by now we were in a tiny side room and about eight or nine of us were pushing and jostling to find a hook for our coats, and then a place in front of the small unframed mirror.

I stood and watched them twist curls round their fingers, dab powder puffs over already heavily coated cheeks and noses, lips were re-glossed and then as the one and only chair became vacant, their outdoor shoes were replaced by twinkling silver and gold dance sandals.

It was the latter that started my evening of despair. I didn't mind not having any make-up or my hair unpermed, but what would I have given to have stepped out into Our Lady of Grace's hall in a pair of those sandals!

However, in retrospect, I am sure they would have made no difference, for the rest of the evening I was invisible to all. Marjorie introduced me to Donald, who immediately swept her off down the hall in a series of intricate dance-steps. I was now absolutely scared out of my life in case any boy did ask me to dance, for as I watched I knew that I could never get my feet to glide along and cross over and backwards like that. After each dance Marjorie came back to me and Donald went back to his gang of boys. She pointed out people she had met at other dances and urged me to have a go at the next Ladies Excuse-Me, but by now I was firmly embedded into a shoulder-hunching wall-leaning position and I only moved when it was interval time and we both went to a trestle table at the far end of the hall and bought ourselves a glass of orange squash.

The second half of the evening followed the same nightmare pattern. My eyes were drawn to the clock, again and again, as if its hands were a magnet and my pupils made of steel. Through the smoky haze I saw that it had stopped and it still said a quarter to ten, the same as it had when I looked at it an hour or so ago ... surely by now it must be eleven o'clock and time to go home. Looking around the room to see where Marjorie was I caught sight of the clock again. It now said ten o'clock. Realising that I had made a mistake all I could now do was to stand and pray the minutes away.

Marjorie was getting so upset and desperately tried to make me walk to another part of the hall.

"No-one can see you standing there, walk down to the corner near the band. It will be the last waltz soon, you can't stay here by yourself for that."

But I did - at least for the start of it and then I slid, unnoticed, hugging the wall, step by step until the haven of the cloakroom was reached. There I waited for Marjorie.

She was very kind to me and took my arm tightly as we walked home - her other arm was held by Donald, who was far from pleased with my company.

I left them both at the corner of the street and hastily said goodnight as I stumbled over the cobbles to my own home, the second to last house at the top of the street. My feet ached with standing, and I longed for the privacy of my bed, but I knew there was one more thing to do before that happy state was reached.

I made a great show of putting the big iron key in the front door and the light coming from beneath the kitchen door told me that Mum and Dad had, as I expected, brought friends back from the pub for supper.

I popped my head round the door, "Hi", I said, they all looked up from the table.

"Going straight up to bed - I'm worn out, it's been super", I grinned at them.

Dad grinned back, "Enjoy yourself Blossom? That's the ticket, enjoy yourself."

Mum smiled too, "Was it a good dance love?"

I nodded.

"That's nice, I'm glad", she said.

CHAPTER THIRTY ONE

Part of my job was taking orders from the girls on the bench for their elevenses. The huge works canteen was situated across the front yard and I soon learned to push and shove my way to the counter and start reeling off my list of cheese rolls, chocolate swiss rolls, eccles cakes and the favourite, cheese cake, which had no connection with cheese in any way, consisting entirely of pastry, soft cake filling iced over the top with sugar and sprinkled with long coconut sugared strands.

It was here at the canteen that I met up with other red-light girls and also the messenger girls. These latter I soon found out were a step up from us. Where as we ran up and down grabbing tins and screws from the bench, they worked in the offices for the staff, and they ran all over the place, other buildings, factory shops, stores, even sometimes into the directors' offices. They carried papers, drawings and important looking envelopes, and conducted official visitors to various parts of the factory. Their hours were of course staff hours, nine to five but now and again they would have to either come in earlier or stay later and it had been one of these messenger girls who had met me on my first morning and shown me where L Building was.

I saw this girl most days at the canteen and she always had a smile and cheery greeting for me. I felt flattered that someone from the staff spoke to me and I looked forward to seeing her.

She was was very pretty, her hair bounced about in little curls and she usually wore a small velvet bow on the top of her head. Her eyes seemed to be perpetually laughing, and her rosy cheeks belonged more to a country girl, she positively glowed and always looked as if she was bursting with energy. She never seemed to walk, always ran, laughing and shouting out wise-cracks to the workmen or apprentices in the tool-shop doorway. Her clothes were very modern and to me she looked like an American college girl straight from the movies.

One morning I noticed her in front of me getting served with the requirements of her office colleagues; as she turned from the counter she saw me and to my surprise waited until I too had been served. We walked back down the road together to the junction where I turned right for my factory shop and she went left towards the big office block. Before leaving she said that they had a vacancy in her office for a messenger and why didn't I go after it.

I was too stunned to speak - another job. I had given up all thoughts of doing anything but factory work. But now that this wonderful offer had been temptingly placed before me I realised how easily my ambitions had fallen by the wayside. I eagerly took in the marvellous illuminating words gaily tripping from her ruby red lips ... "we could work together, I'd show you around, it's easy, and you get to know all the boys. I'll tell Miss Wilson about you if you like ..."

With my mind in a whirl I fled back to L Building and hardly noticed the swearing and scolding I got for bringing back the girls' elevenses too late for them to be eaten. I wondered vaguely during my dinner hour if I had actually said yes or no to my friend. Feeling like a stupid dolt instead of the usual picture of myself as a bright imaginative misunderstood genius I steadily worked through the afternoon planning what I would say to her when we met tomorrow morning in the canteen.

I leaned by the side of one of Nora's boxes, not really seeing her place the various articles of telephone equipment on to the belt; I was making up grateful sentences of acceptance, ready for the morning. A sharp jolt from Nora's elbow brought me round in time to realise that Mr Andrews the shop foreman was bearing down on me. Apart from speaking to me on my first day and handing out my weekly wage packet Mr Andrews and I could have been in two different worlds. He was the boss and I was so low down in the pecking order of the factory floor that there was no reason for us to meet up during the day, let alone speak to each other. And so when he stopped by my side and asked me to go into his office with him I walked in his shadow, trembling and wondering just what I had done wrong.

To my amazement he told me to sit down in the chair opposite his and then, very gently, he spoke. "So you want to leave us then."

I felt my eyes growing bigger and my tongue grow smaller ... I wondered how he knew about it, but I just couldn't find the power to speak. He continued, "well why not try to better yourself, I reckon you've earned it, you have been a good girl to me so run off now and see Miss Wilson in the P. P. D. office and see if you can be a good girl for her." Still without saying a word I rose from the chair and left the office, but he still had another surprise for me, for at the door he tapped me on the shoulder.

"Good luck little 'un", he smiled.

If my first day at the factory had scared me the feelings as I walked down the long corridor towards the P . P . D . office were terrifying. What on earth was I doing here, alongside the staff. The ones who didn't wear overalls, the ones who obviously wore their best clothes to work everyday.

I watched doors opening and shutting, people walking up and down, going in and out of offices. There were so many doors and they all looked alike. I heard little bursts from typewriters as I passed half opened doors. Telephones rang, people spoke, laughed, shouted even. But I was aware of an atmosphere that was different, here there was no hum of machinery, no tools banging down on to benches, no women's voices humming and singing the latest popular melodies high above the incessant din rising from the factory floors. This atmosphere I liked.

There were four doors on the left-hand side of the corridor and they all had P. P. D. written on them.

I decided on the second one and cautiously knocked. No-one answered and so I opened the door slowly and looked in. I don't know what I really expected, never having been inside a huge office block before, but I could see why no-one had heard my knock. There were simply masses of people sitting at desks in a huge room that seemed to go on forever. I thought there must be hundreds of them, but I found out afterwards that it was about eighty. I saw too that all four doors led into this office.

In the centre of all the hub-bub were two rows of desks which had typewriters on them and typists busily banging away with flying fingers over unlooked-at keys. And sitting at a small desk at the end of one of the rows was my new friend. She had large piles of papers in front of her and looking over the top of these she saw me and signalled with her eyes towards a smartly dressed woman who was looking at one of the typists' work. Miss Wilson? I mouthed. Yes, came a nod of the head. I approached the typists' section and stood at the end of the first row and Miss Wilson saw me. She gave me a smile and I followed her to her own desk, in the middle of the typists.

So I would like to be a messenger girl? Did I know that it was very hard work, not only running all over the place but also helping with the office filing and any other little job that needed doing. I only knew that I had to work in this office, I would have given anything to have stayed there right away and never gone back to L Building. I felt the office atmosphere enveloping me, I was smothered by it and loved it. I nodded eagerly to all her questions; no, I never got tired running about, my legs never ached and although I had no idea what she meant about filing I told her I could do that as well. Anything, I pleaded inside of me, I'll do anything if only I can get this job.

All right, she said, I was to be the new messenger girl. However there was one snag. I would have to stay classified as I was, I could not transfer to Staff. This meant my hours would not be nine to five but remain as they were. Never mind, she continued, there would be plenty for me to do in those extra hours and of course I would get the same salary as the other messengers which was fifteen shillings a week.

I had given no thought to extra wages, and the joy of an extra half-a-crown a week far outweighed the slight cloud of not being Staff.

Reaction to my news at home was mixed. Dad could not see why I was not satisfied with the job I already had.

"You'll soon find out your face doesn't fit", he said, "you will never be one of them. Look how they have refused to make you Staff, and that's just the start. No, my girl, there's no place for you among that lot."

But Fred wished he had found a friend like mine and I was to make the most of it. Mum was frightened in case they decided against keeping me after a while - would I get my old job back again? "Of course I wouldn't," said Dad, "did I think a job would be kept open just for the likes of me?"

The extra half-a-crown was however given slight praise and I think that in order to make up for the nasty things that Dad said over and over again, Mum told me that I could keep all of it for myself, in order she added to dress more smartly for work.

And so began my transition away from the factory floor and into the realms of office life. By starting at a quarter to eight I spent most of the early hours with the cleaners, while I learned how to file and topped up the inkwells. I found it harder than I thought to forget that I was still rated factory and that my staff status was with a small 's'.

My new friend's name was Barbara but everyone called her Babs, even Miss Wilson ! She took me under her wing and although only a year older than me she seemed so very grown up and self assured.

The office took some sorting out, first I had to learn the names of the heads of the inter-office departments and then the different groups doing what seemed to be an endless variety of jobs. The desks were three or four abreast stretching across from the very large windows and the room was divided into its several sections not by partitions but by the type of work done in each area.

At the top end were two rows of accounts under the eagle eye of Mr Berry. Then there was one row of invoice checkers. Next came the typing pool, ten typists working under the supervision of Miss Wilson, plus of course two messenger girls. The lower part of the office was given over to those mysterious people called progress chasers.

My job entailed taking papers, memos, and drawings to and from all parts of the factory and as this covered several acres of land stretching from the main Woolwich road down to the river and included various buildings containing offices, laboratories, stores, factory workshops, not to mention the fire-station, first aid wing, canteen, staff dining room, porter's lodges - I soon realised how true Miss Wilson's words had been. How my legs ached. My red light job had allowed sitting down in between times with nothing to do but look for red lights. But now when I returned from the Iron Mill shop on the far side of the site it was only to find I was required to pick some papers up from the Battery shop which was away over on the opposite side.

But once inside a place like the Battery shop I knew how lucky I really was. I hated the place, it frightened me. Everything was black, a fine soot covered the floor, benches, even the windows were so grimy that little if any daylight seeped through. The women wore long overalls almost to their feet, and scarves, caps and turbans covered their hair completely. I watched them as they filled the zinc battery cases with pitch, hot and steamy like treacle, whilst at the far end of the room the heat was almost unbearable - I never went down to that end. The air was heavy with the smell of the pitch, and the thumping and clanging of the heavy machinery, along with the barrels of pitch being rolled over the stone floors turned the whole scene into a nightmare. As I walked through the long dark room towards the small glass office I felt the heat seeping through my clothes. I hoped the papers would be ready and waiting, and that I would not have to stand inside that square glass box feeling like a trapped animal. From inside that office the people outside looked like a lot of black ants scurrying and hurrying, lifting huge loads of zinc cases, or completed cardboard boxes of torch batteries. They obviously carried on conversations by lip reading as the noise made it impossible to hear what anyone said and even inside the office it was necessary to raise your voice to be heard.

Once back outside the Battery shop I took big gulps of fresh air and thanked my lucky stars I was a messenger girl.

I soon settled down into my new life, loving all of it. To have my own desk made me feel very proud and although I was shy of using the telephone at first this soon became an everyday thing. But it was the typewriters that fascinated me and at lunch-time and during the dinner hour I was allowed to practise, supervised by either Miss Wilson or one of the typists. In a few weeks Miss Wilson said I definitely had an aptitude for it and she advised me to start evening classes to learn properly. Immediately my old ambition of educating myself came flooding back, how could I have ever given up so easily?

In September I enrolled for the commercial course at the school in Blackheath Hill, the very school where I had tried to further my education at the outset of war. But now I was a fully paid up pupil starting on a new career with the commercial course.

My new world of work led to a new world of play. Babs lived within walking distance of Siemens and shortly after I started my new job she invited me home to tea. I was quickly accepted by Mom, as Babs' mother was known to all her friends, and I soon became one of the regular crowd belonging to Babs' local cycling and social club. They held monthly dances in a hut in Church Lane, Charlton and I was invited to the very next one. As it did not finish until after my last tram had gone Babs suggested I stay the night at her home.

Whilst I packed a small brown cardboard suitcase with my nightdress, slippers, toothbrush and flannel, on the Saturday afternoon, Mum fussed about as if I was going to the moon, and well she might. It was the first time that I had ever slept away from home and so at nearly fifteen years of age I became really excited as I felt like a grown-up for the first time.

114

CHAPTER THIRTY TWO

For a few weeks I walked to work as the main road had been bombed between Greenwich and Charlton making it impossible for trams to run although a few buses did manage still to get through. I enjoyed walking the couple of miles each morning along with the workers from the Kork'n'seal Factory, the Rope Works, the Glass Factory and Harvey's Steel Works. Dad accompanied me as far as Lombard Lane where he turned off on to the towpath, continuing his last mile by the side of the river. A nice walk in summer but treacherous on dark winter mornings when frost made walking along the narrow path very difficult, but Dad had done it year in and year out since he was fourteen and he could have found his way along it with his eyes shut.

I enjoyed these morning walks with Dad, and we would talk together like real companions. He loved his work and was sorry that our Fred had given up boat-building - he was not happy either about the apprentices under him, saying they had neither brains nor interest to carry on with the great traditions of barge-building. But to give Dad due, he thought well of Fred now that he had proved himself in his new career in electrical engineering.

Fred and his fiance Pam were to be married at Christmas and to my delight I was to be a bridesmaid. What a year this was - a new job, more money to spend and a bridesmaid as well. Pam was determined that the war was not going to spoil her wedding day and St Mary's Church in Woolwich was booked for the event. It was to be a grand affair I realised, as she excitedly chatted about her long white velvet dress and mine, which was to be a similar design in red velvet.

The dresses were made by an elderly grey-haired lady, who lived in Charlton Village. I was fascinated to see her hobbling round my feet, her mouth full of pins, and still being able to answer Pam's many queries about length, waist-line, fullness of sleeves, and all the time she turned up hems, put in pins, pulled out other pins, pinched and pleated, with her bun of thin hair gradually escaping from its nest of hair pins. But how grand I felt in that gently swirling glowing velvet. I wondered whose clothing coupons had been used but I was quickly shut up by Pam and her mother. One of Pam's aunties had a stall in Beresford Square, Woolwich and it was a well known fact that no-one in 'trade' went without anything, war or no war. They had no fear about me talking . . . I had learned very young to keep quiet about what went on around me.

There was no chance of them getting a home of their own for a year or more as so many houses had been bombed. They were going to have a room in Pam's mother's house.

After one of our dressmaking sessions Pam suddenly said, "what about your hair?"

"Well, what about it?"

"I can't have you looking like that - you look as if you still go to school. You'll have to have it permed."
Mum agreed and offered to pay for it as well so there was nothing I could do about it. Two weeks before the great day I found myself trembling a little as I sat in a curtained cubicle and waited for Madam Christy to start on my thick short straight hair.

I got the giggles when I saw myself attached to the perming machine by wires and curlers, but Madam Christy looked so sternly at me that I sat quietly through the rest of the procedure.

When I looked in the mirror at the finished result I wanted to cry. There looking back at me was a round shiny red face, surrounded by rows and rows and rows of frizzy curls. They stuck out all round my head making me look like a Zulu warrior. Madam Christy was shaking her head and glared at me,

"It's so thick, and you took twice as long as you should have done under the drier." I was speechless, but she went on, "I have never had such a head before", and then she realised I suppose just what I was feeling and she continued, "never mind, it will be better after the first set."

Mum had made me take a scarf to the hairdresser's in case it rained and was I glad I had it. I tied it tight around my now even thicker, bouncy hair and ran home, back along Trafalgar Road. I did not stop until safe inside our front door, I would have died if any of my friends had seen me.

As I pulled off the scarf I watched Mum's eyes get rounder and rounder, she was dumb at the sight of me, but Dad wasn't and putting the blame entirely on me, he yelled,

"What the hell have you been and done to yourself, you look like a bleedin' mad woman. Go and comb it all out, do you hear me, I won't have you walking about like that."

But even Dad's authority was flouted when it came to my hair ... for nothing would make it stay down flat. It was impossible to get a comb through the mass of frizz and if I brushed it then it just sprang up even more. I panicked - how could I get out of looking like this? Of course it was impossible for me to go to work. I started to cry and shouted at Mum, "You think of something, you made me have the perm in the first place."

And then Dad told me off for shouting at Mum. What with me crying, Dad cursing and banging about the kitchen none of us heard the front door shut as Fred and Pam walked in. Fred just collapsed with laughter but Pam was furious, she too blamed me entirely.

"What on earth did you let them do that to you for. Go straight back and get them to put it right."

But I flatly refused, nothing would get me back inside Madam Christy's again, and eventually Pam took pity on me and with a bowl of water and Dad's own comb with longer teeth she managed to make me look a bit more human, but only until it dried, and then it just sprang up again into a ball of frizz.

Naturally there was no getting out of going to work on Monday and for once I was glad that I started earlier than all the others. When they came in I had moved my desk into a corner away from its usual place by the window, and surrounded by stacks of papers to file it was some little while before my plight became the focus of whistles and cat-calls, and more than one pair of eyebrows were raised when I walked by. But Babs told me that her hair went like that when it was first permed and it would be much better after the first set. And so I lived through that most uncomfortable week until Friday when Mum firmly marched me back to Madam Christy for a shampoo and set. I had to admit it looked a little better at the end of the session, but I never liked myself again until my hair grew long enough to have most of the frizz cut off. Pam was very upset, saying I would spoil her wedding and I was worried in case she decided not to have me as a bridesmaid. But then I remembered the dress and was glad I was small for once. There was no-one in either family that the dress would fit so it had to be me, frizzy hair and all.

Little did we know that troubles like wrong hair-dos were indeed of complete insignificance compared to what happened just three days before the wedding. Pam's mother's house was bombed, and although thankfully no lives were lost, the entire wedding wardrobe, the wedding presents and of course their home were completely destroyed. This event made us all think a bit more deeply about what was going on around us ... but not for long. Dad would not let anyone be miserable, not with his son's wedding in a couple of days time. All the stops were pulled out, all friends called in help ... everything was to continue as planned ... well nearly as planned.

Pam wore a blue woollen coat and a saucy little hat pulled over one eye, and I was in an apple green skirt and jacket. It did not matter that colours clashed, and thankfully my frizzy hair was concealed by a scarf as no hat would stay perched perilously on top of my ever bouncing rows of sausages. The air-aid warning went during the service and we heard bombs falling across the river near the docks. The wedding reception had been hastily re-arranged and was now held in the Catholic Club Hall near Woolwich Arsenal Station. Pam's family were Catholics but she had not married in a catholic church and I am sure Dad would not have gone if she had insisted upon this.

During the reception, after drinks had been passed around a few times Dad got on to the subject of religion and became quite abusive in his remarks to Pam's mother. She of course was upset and I wondered if this wedding would turn out like our sister Daisy's with both families shouting and arguing, but Fred quite calmly took over the whole affair and soon the talk changed from religion to the usual dirty jokes about wedding nights.

I wonder what Dad would say if he were alive to see that same hall today - it's a Sikh Temple!

CHAPTER THIRTY THREE

After Fred's marriage Mum told me that I could move my things into the front bedroom, and so for the very first time that I could remember there was somewhere for me to go and be alone, to sit and read, or write another highly dramatic story, or just to try and do something with my hair. I had started to use make-up and spent hours in front of the mirrors of the dressing table experimenting with face powder, rouge and lipstick.

Thankfully my hair was growing and the weight of it was beginning to help flatten out the frizz from the perm.

Best of all in having my own room was that I could now have Marjorie come and spend evenings with me. She often spent an hour or so with me talking about clothes and film stars and boy-friends. At least Marjorie talked about boy-friends, I had still to meet my very first one.

Her great ambition at this time was to be a champion ballroom dancer and she had lessons regularly. When she went dancing at the Town Hall in Greenwich or the New Cross Palais she met and danced with the partners she knew from her dancing classes. Marjorie tried hard to get me to go to dances with her but the evening when I had been such a wallflower at Our Lady of Grace Hall in Charlton had never been repeated.

However she was determined and pointed out that now I earned more money I could afford to join the ballroom dancing school. She was sure that I would learn the steps very quickly, and it was a good way to meet boys she said.

So far I was not a success with the boys. When I went to Babs' social evenings at her cycling club she always introduced me to a gang of boys, but somehow by her side I soon became invisible and although I was not left out, neither was I picked out as special by anyone. I became resigned to being the girl who looked after her companion's handbag whilst she danced, or kept a seat for her at the cafe whilst she arranged a date for the next cycling trip.

I had twenty-five shillings saved up in the Post Office and with seven and sixpence of this I bought what was to be the first of many pairs of silver, gold, flat-heeled, high-heeled, twinkling, buckled, shiny buttoned, gloriously luxurious fairyland footwear ... dancing sandals.

For Marjorie was right, from that first Saturday afternoon when I entered the long oblong room, with mirrors from ceiling to floor down one side of it, and I smelt the warm, dusty, chalky atmosphere, and heard Victor Sylvester's Strict Tempo Dance Orchestra coming from the gramophone standing on a table in the corner, I was well and truly hooked. I eagerly listened to the gentle voice of Miss Baxter, the principal of the dancing school, explaining the tangle of steps that miraculously turned themselves into the fox-trot or quick-step - especially when guided by Miss Baxter herself, her firm hand on your shoulder somehow conveyed the right instructions to your feet.

The exhilaration of executing a cross-chassis with a fish-tail in the quick-step, the soft cocoon of glamour that enveloped me as I lay back against my partner's hold and glided into the slow fox-trot and when I had mastered the perfect heel-turn in this romantic dance I was overjoyed. But there was more to come ... the fun of doing the rhumba, the haughty serious expression one learned to put on when performing the tango, very serious the tango. But I loved every minute of it and meeting Jim was of course the peak of my enjoyment.

He was a tall gangling blonde boy of seventeen and he joined the classes the same day as I did and although I hardly reached to his shoulder Miss Baxter decided we should partner each other from the start. Jim was very shy and when I knew him better it astonished me that he had ever plucked up enough nerve to come along for lessons.

After three weeks he asked me if I would be going to the Town Hall Dance that same Saturday night and I said yes. Marjorie had a date for the dance and during our weekly bathing session at the municipal baths we excitedly chatted about dresses, make-up and perfume and of course boys.

Back home I showed her my new brown pleated skirt and she insisted that I wear one of her blouses made in coffee coloured lace with huge bishop sleeves gathered into a tight wristband. She even managed to do something to my hair by damping it down with sugar water and rolling it in some pipe cleaners.

Even I liked the look of the girl facing me in the mirror this time. I had a generous supply of Ponds lipstick and I dabbed from my new block of solid face powder which had been a birthday present from Mum, giving cheeks and nose a plentiful covering. I was still faithful to my California Poppy perfume and liberally applied this to ears, wrists, blouse, hair and, a new idea from one of the typist's magazines at work ... a piece of cotton wool thoroughly soaked with the perfume and tucked in between what I hopefully called my bust. How I envied Marjorie with her already developed figure, especially her hips on which her skirts swung provocatively, whilst I still went straight up and down.

However nothing was going to spoil this night for me, I could dance and I had a partner waiting for me ... and as I came out of the Ladies cloakroom I saw Jim in his dark blue suit, black patent shoes, his blonde hair smoothly Brylcreemed and gleaming ... and he was waiting for me, I almost ran straight into his arms then and there in the foyer, but recovered myself in good time and casually walked over to him, chatting unconcernedly with Marjorie as we went.

I danced every dance with Jim and only saw Marjorie momentarily either whirling past or walking back to one group or another. We met up for the interval, just the four of us, Jim and me and Marjorie with one of her partners, and we had a drink in a pub in Royal Hill.

The last waltz was as romantic as I had dreamed. I leaned against Jim and he hummed, "Who's taking you Home Tonight" and then suddenly it was all over and I was among a pressing chattering crowd of girls in the cloakroom. Giggling, whispering, discussing who was going home with who. After grabbing coats, changing shoes and another quick flick of the powder puff plus a shake of California Poppy, it was time to find our escorts.

The four of us who had spent the interval together found ourselves walking home together. The black-out was in force but as yet no raid had started, it would not be long however before the sirens sounded as it was a regular nightly routine. As we walked back through Greenwich Park, past the lovely white house that had once belonged to a queen, I felt Jim's arm tighten around me and the excitement that started to quickly flow through me was just as quickly replaced by fear. I had read about people kissing, falling in love even, but until now that was the whole of my sex education. Instinct told me that I was about to be kissed and I wanted an excuse to turn my head away ... I stopped to take an imaginary stone from my shoe and the moment passed. At last we were at the corner of my street. The four of us stood awkardly apart and then Marjorie's boyfriend took her firmly by the arm and steered her towards the gate in the wall which led to her home. They both said goodnight to Jim and me and got no reply. I knew then that he was as scared as I was. I looked up at him, he was so tall, "I live right at the top of the street, last house but one." He glanced up the dark narrow cobbles, suddenly the air raid sirens shrieked and almost immediately we heard the rocket guns firing and the heavy drone of aircraft overhead.

"Quick," Jim grabbed my hand and we ran together into the darkness of the street. It was suddenly fun and we started to laugh as we ran ... too late I remembered the sandbags left out on the doorsteps and I found myself flying through the air as I ran into those outside Mrs Allen's. But before I reached the ground I felt myself lifted up by two strong arms which set me on my feet then crept around my shoulders and pulled me closer and closer. It was just like one of the magazine stories, only our lips didn't quite meet properly the first time ... more like my nose on his chin.

The bombing became quite heavy but Jim refused to take up the offer of sharing our air raid shelter as his mother would be worried. Half an hour later I lay on my bunk reliving not only my first two kisses, but all the dances, the way we had almost flown down the length of the hall in the quick-step, and the perfect match we had been in the waltz. And lastly I wondered if next week he would ask me to the dance again . . . and maybe meet me outside the Town Hall this time and I would then not have to pay for myself.

CHAPTER THIRTY FOUR

Marjorie now had a steady boyfriend and it made me realise that being a grown-up took something more than just learning to dance and getting your first kiss. When I told her that I still didn't quite feel part of the adult world she said that my troubles came from worrying too much, I should forget all my fears about not dressing like everyone else, or not wanting to dance with a particular boy because he was too tall - I should go out and just enjoy myself. Well it was easy to tell me this, but it made no real difference ... until the evening in, of all places, Our Lady of Grace Hall. That wretched dance hall that had given me so much misery.

I had been back there several times and it was different now because I had become confident. Not only could I dance but several of the other dancers knew me. There was one particular boy who attracted much attention from all the girls - I only knew that his name was Tony, but oh how I longed to dance with him. He was so smooth, so good looking, dressed smartly and was a marvellous dancer. I had noticed that at most dances there was always a boy like this and all the girls fell over each other in the ladies excuse-me dance to dance with him. But this boy, here at Our Lady of Grace, he did all the picking and choosing and he seemed so sophisticated that I never had the courage to approach him during the excuse-me dances. I did however always try to make my steps fit my partners with expert precision when we passed him, hoping he would be impressed by my exquisite heel-turn and ask for the next dance. But usually he stood on one side and his eyes roamed the hall and although I would try and will them to stop on me, they passed on to rest on someone much luckier than me.

During pauses between dances I forced myself not to look at him and joined my usual group of friends. One evening, from the corner of my eye, I saw him slowly walk over and I started to tremble, I knew he was coming over to me. The band started up, it was a waltz, how I would show off my newly learned step, the hesitation and turn ... and then just as he reached the edge of our group I felt a very slight touch on my elbow from behind. Turning round I saw a stocky boy in RAF uniform. His face a deep red which showed his black hair up even darker, he looked awkward and kept running his hand through his hair again and again. He shyly asked me to dance and I felt more like giving him a kick ... how could he! I wanted to cry I was so angry. How dare he! And then I noticed my glamorous would-be partner. He was grinning down at both of us and with a lift of his eye-brows at the stuttering boy in uniform he pointed to the badge representing half a wing on his breastpocket. "What happened to the other half of the plane then, did you lose it?" and he laughed and walked away. I felt so sorry for the airman that I found myself taking hold of his hand and leading him out on to the floor, to the cheers of my friends.

Too late I realised that not only was he unable to dance, but that he was still wearing his RAF issue boots, and my romantic waltz finished up with a broken buckle on my new sandal and a hole in one precious silk stocking. But I didn't care. All I suddenly cared about was being with Johnny. We sat out most of the other dances and I found out that although he lived quite near to me he had gone to a school on the other side of Greenwich.

He was very proud to be in the Air Force and I think he said he was a navigator, or perhaps it was a rear gunner ... it didn't matter what he was, all I knew was that at last I had met that very special someone. I could not believe it when the last waltz was announced, where had the time gone to? We shuffled very inexpertly around the hall, but only as far as the cloakroom where I speedily collected my coat. None of the gang were surprised when we left the hall arm in arm shouting out our goodnights behind us. Johnny walked me right up to my front door and it seemed perfectly natural for me to find myself in his arms. He had a long week-end leave due the following week and we arranged to meet outside the New Cross Cinema on Friday night. I went indoors smiling my secret to myself.

CHAPTER THIRTY FIVE

Things were changing at the office. Babs was promoted to the Drawing Office and a new messenger girl arrived on the scene.

When the new girl arrived I resented having to explain why I worked different hours, it was still a big chip on my shoulder to be rated as factory and not staff. Within the company status the new girl, being staff, was in a higher grade than me, but in physical terms I was the Senior Messenger Girl. There was however a miracle that helped to overcome any inferior feelings I had. This new girl was smaller than me! At last I could stretch my five foot nothing above her as we walked the different parts of the factory and I airily explained the work to her.

But I could not keep it up for long, she was such a quiet pathetic little creature, very shy and timid. Soon during our walks she started to tell me about herself. Her name was Jane and she was an orphan. All her life had been spent in a children's home where although looked after kindly by the housemother she had found it difficult to mix in with the other boisterous children. At fourteen years of age the home not only obtained this job for her but also her lodgings.

It was her new home that excited her the most, every day she told me about the motherly landlady and her husband and I soon knew every detail of her own room, right down to the last photograph of the landlady's grandchildren which stood on the mantlepiece.

She had been with us about six weeks when the 'dreadful scene' as Miss Wilson called it occurred. Just after dinner Jane complained about pains in her stomach and earlier in the day she had told me that her head ached. Miss Wilson sent her along to see the nurse and I started the afternoon routine of collecting copy invoices from the stores. This usually took about an hour and so I was surprised to find that Jane had not returned to the office when I got back. Miss Wilson telephoned the first-aid building and was told that Jane had been given some aspirin and was having a lie down. She would probably be well enough to return to the office in half an hour. It was decided to send me down and await to accompany her.

Nurse seemed glad to see me and said that she had found Jane in a very nervous state and had hardly been able to get any response from her questions about her general state of health. She gathered that the poor child was having a rather bad period and was too embarrassed to speak about it. This was nothing unusual, I myself never mentioned how I felt when I too had a period. It was a subject never mentioned in the grown-up world at large.

Before leaving the sick bay Jane was given some more aspirins and an extra large sanitary towel and advised to put this on before going home, and nurse added, she was sure the headache would soon be better.

On our way back to the office Jane left me to go into the ladies cloakroom and I went on ahead to explain the situation to Miss Wilson. I had just finished when we heard a gasp, followed by giggles and lots of HHMM! ! HHHMMM! ! from the older men, and turning round we saw the incredible spectacle of Jane walking towards us with the sanitary towel across her forehead with the loops over her ears ... Miss Wilson screamed before rushing up to the poor girl and pushing her out of the room and out of sight of the now helpless crowd in the office who with tears streaming down their faces lay doubled up with laughter across their desks. All of them that is except two of the lady typists who were very red and stubbornly looked down at their machines.

Poor Jane - she was even more ignorant than I had been. We might be in 1941, we could see the latest American movie, and wear modern short skirts, and jitterbug, drink and smoke BUT we did not talk about things like periods.

The embarrassment was too much and she was transferred to another part of the works. Eventually another job in a different factory was found for her.

I was now the only messenger girl in the office and I wondered if this might be an excuse for promoting me to staff. But the answer was no and my pride took a nasty jolt. From that time on there was a niggling dissatisfaction with my job.

It was my godmother, Aunt Dora, who helped to solve my problem. Now that there was a war on, she had decided to do her bit and she worked at a cable factory in Greenwich. The irony of this was that whereas my Mum who had worked full-time in the rope factory all her life and now due to ill health worked part-time was still a plain factory hand - Aunt Dora who had never worked before was busy climbing the career ladder and had already been made a charge-hand with the prospect soon of becoming a forewoman.

" It's who you know, not what you know", she told me when I confided bitterly to her about my troubles at the office. "You would be better off starting new, somewhere else."

I agreed, "But where could I go? I was lucky to get this office job, I haven't any exams behind me."

"You can type though, and you must know other office work by now. I heard our manager saying that they will have to get more staff in our Buying Department soon ... you know we're that busy now and yet apparently the firm was almost bust a couple of years back. 'S funny ain't it, when you think that this war' as done someone a bit of good."

"Do you reckon I could get this job with you?"

"Not with me love, I'm no office worker. No, you would have to go over to the Labour Exchange."

The jobs come through them now, war work, that's what we are, see. You can't even get in our place without a green card from them anyway."

I did not want to go to the Labour Exchange, it would have meant losing a day from work which would have to be explained to Mum. Somehow or other that Buying Office job remained in my mind and within a day or so I had decided upon a plan.

The following Monday morning, although I left home at the usual time, I did not go to work. As soon as I got off the tram at Charlton I hung around until most of the other workers had gone through the gates of the factory, then I ran across the road and took another tram back home.

I had to walk up and down the main road in case anyone saw me returning and as soon as it was clear I ran up the street and indoors.

I quickly changed into my best skirt and blouse before leaving home again and heading straight across the main road, down Christchurch Street to the gates of the cable factory.

I asked the gatekeeper the way to the Buying Department and he asked me for my green card. Glad for once to be small I tried looking sad and said that I had lost it.

"Well now what are we going to do - I reckon you'll just have to go back and get another."

"But the job might go to someone else by the time I get back - my Aunt Dora works here, can't you let me in?"

"No, you might be a spy", and he laughed down at me, then said "I know you, don't I, you live at the top of the alley, what they call Woodland Street."

"Yes", I gasped eagerly.

"All right then, just this once ... turn left at the end of this road, then right and left again. The building on the edge of the river. Good luck, but for Gawd's sake don't let them know how you got in ... you know that they will ask for your green card, don't you ? "

But I did not care ... I was in.

The buying department was in three rooms on the ground floor and in answer to my knock I found myself in a rather dark, but spacious office. There were only three desks and at two of them sat young women, one a very tall elegant blonde and the other who was now coming towards me who wore her hair in a rather old fashioned style, smoothed into a long roll at the back, but she had a beautiful smile. She was the Chief Buyer's personal secretary and gave me a short interview before taking me through the next office where the assistant buyer worked, and finally showed me into the office of the Chief Buyer himself. She gave me a little push on the shoulder before smiling, "Good luck".

I found myself in front of a huge desk, my feet sinking into deep carpet, whilst a pair of steely eyes pierced through thick pebble lens, straight into mine.

I knew immediately that my plan had failed. I could never lie my way past this man. For one thing he terrified me, he was so huge, sitting there like a massive block of granite, hands clenched on the desk top. "What's your name?".

I told him.

"So you want to work here eh! ! WHY?" His voice matched his frame, he roared. I started to mutter, he told me to speak up.

"I think it would be nice to work here".

"NICE", he roared again ... "What do you know about a buying department?"

"I can type".

"I have typists".

"I can file".

"Where did you file?" he seemed to sneer. I told him and it went on and on, question and answer, until somehow or other he had got most of my story out of me . . . all except the bit about the green card and as he hadn't mentioned it I began to feel safe. There were more questions about my commercial course and finally he leaned back and said, "All right, leave me your green card and I'll let you know."

It had come at last. I gulped, but stood my ground.

"I haven't got one".

He sat upright, his eyes tore through me as his hands crashed down on to the desk.

"What! Well then little one, how the hell did you get in here?"

I thought he would be capable of tearing both Aunt Dora and the gateman from limb to limb if I mentioned them so I just said that I dodged in whilst a lorry was being checked. Still not satisfied he continued, "And how did you know we had a vacancy?" My explanation of overhearing a conversation in the fish and chip shop was met with a withering look as he dismissed me. I walked back home with a heavy heart. Not only a job lost but a day's pay as well. How to explain that to Mum on Friday night.

The next evening we were having tea when a double rat-tat sounded on our door. It not only made our cups rattle but Mum went pale and Dad spilling tea from his saucer swore profusely and marched up the passage just in time to get a second volley in his face. He almost tore the door off its hinges as he opened it to find not only a telegram boy but a crowd of curious neighbours as well.

Telegrams were messengers of doom, especially in war-time but we had no-one in the forces and that made the neighbours wonder why we had one. Dad grabbed the envelope, took one look at it and banged the door shut. As he walked back down the passage he yelled "Now what you been up to?" It was for me.

126

I had never ever seen one before let alone held one and I trembled so much that Dad grabbed it again and tore it open.

"What's all this then my girl?"

I read the telegram, it said "Like your cheek. The job is yours." Signed Mr Lakey, Buying Department. I could have jumped over the moon ... I had obtained a real office job. I could hardly wait until tea was over and I rushed down to Marjorie to tell her the good news. When I returned home Daisy was there and Mum had just given her the telegram to read. She looked grim and Mum started to cry, "I don't know what will become of her. Where does she get it all from? You and Fred were never like this. Why can't she settle? Such a nice job you got her at Siemens, but no she gave herself airs and had to go into that office. Now that's not good enough for her, she's off again and now it's telegrams."

Daisy confirmed that I would end up wrong and blamed Mum and Dad for letting me go to ballroom dancing, dance halls were bad places and Daisy was thankful that she had never set foot in one of them. Nothing they said bothered me - I was nearly sixteen years old and had made what I considered the first step towards my goal - deep down inside though I still had no idea just what that goal was.

Two weeks later I started what was to be two very formative years in my working life and once again I realised I had a rise in pay. This time a big jump from fifteen shillings to one guinea a week.

Mr Lakey believed in giving young people as much responsibility as they were willing to take on. And no-one could have been keener than me. Within six months I was travelling to London regularly to deliver to the Ministry of Iron and Steel in Grosvenor Gardens the necessary requisition forms to enable the factory to purchase these metals. I was still really a messenger girl, but now I was doing errands in London and travelling by bus too. As the firm got busier and more orders were being sent out for urgent requirements I took on the job of ringing up suppliers to hurry the completion of these orders. Without realising it I was turned into a progress chaser and one gorgeous morning I arrived in the office to find that we now employed another junior to make the tea and do the filing. I felt proud and I still took these important forms to London regularly.

Mr Lakey continued to frighten me at times, his temper would burst out like a volcano erupting. Quite often he lunched on board one of the cable ships that tied up almost beneath our windows. Once the ship was loaded the Captain usually had a farewell lunch and on these occasions when the boss returned he showed all the signs that Dad did late on a Saturday night. Sometimes he would sack all of us during one of these afternoons but his secretary would simply ring for his chauffeur to take him home. The next morning everything was normal and no-one of course mentioned anything about being sacked. He could be gentle and once or twice he walked along to his car after work and would ask me how I liked the job.

I even found myself telling him about my interests in music and dancing. He always urged me to keep up my reading and introduced me to his two favourite English authors, H. E. Bates and S. P. B. Mais. Sometimes as we talked I imagined him as a father figure, but only until he shouted at me again and glared through those thick pebble lens. But I was always grateful for those years I worked with him.

CHAPTER THIRTY SIX

Most Sunday nights I attended the dances held at New Cross Palais, a very popular place always crowded with gangs of boys and girls, all very clique, keeping within their own groups. Whenever a stranger arrived we all watched to see if any super dancers were among them. If there were we would make sure of showing off our own standard during the excuse-me dances.

One group consisting of three young men all well dressed made a great impact when they first arrived at the Palais. In no time at all the tall sleek boy became the most sought after partner on the floor, not only did he dance beautifully but he looked just like a film star - a smooth, polished Tyrone Power type. He knew this of course and during the next few weeks he had his pick of the bunch with regard to the girls, usually those with super figures in smart clothes.

Marjorie was such an expert dancer that he did actually seek her out for one or two dances most Sundays. Tales soon spread about how much money he spent, he smoked expensive cigarettes and always treated his interval partner to 'shorts' as we called gins, ports or cocktails. Sometimes he and his friends travelled home on the same bus as Marjorie and me and we soon found out that he lived just a little further along the main road towards Charlton.

He always offered us a cigarette during the journey, but I had not started smoking yet although Marjorie had in fact been smoking for a year or more. His sophisticated chatter was miles above my head and I spent most of the journey looking out of the slit by the side of the blackout blind whilst he and Marjorie, along with his two friends, laughed and talked. I was always glad when we reached our bus stop and with a quick "goodnight" to them all I ran downstairs and off the bus.

One of the nice things that occurred at home now was the fact that when I returned from work Mum was there already, with the tea waiting for Dad and me. Since six years of age I had been the one who had returned home first from school and laid the table for the evening meal. Mum was usually finishing off the preparations when I got in but one evening I returned to find her all excited and in a fluster, most unlike her. The tablecloth was not even in sight, she was just sitting and smiling from her armchair when I walked into the kitchen.

"Oh", she smiled, "Why didn't you tell me about him - he's so handsome".

"Who? "

"Arthur, he's been here to see me this afternoon. So polite, and doesn't he carry his clothes well".

"What did he want?"

"He asked if I would give permission for you to go to the pictures with him. Fancy that, what good manners ... a real gentleman". I could not believe it. I spent the rest of the evening telling Mum all the tales I had heard about him at the Palais. She brushed them aside. Dad for once had little to say, but he wondered how Arthur came to be walking the streets in the afternoon. Didn't he bleedin' well have a job? But there was no getting over Mum tonight, she stumped that one too.

"Oh yes, a very good job, something to do with making special measuring instruments I think he said ... he works shifts".

I could see that it was no use arguing, Mum had arranged a date for me with the most notorious man at the Palais!

When the great day arrived I was a bundle of nerves. My hands shook as I applied lipstick and powder. What would we talk about, he must be years older than me ... he arrived punctually and spent a few minutes chatting with Mum and Dad whilst I went to my bedroom for my coat. When I came back downstairs Mum was already at the street door opening it. She positively thrust me out of the house and with Dad stood on the doorstep waving us good bye.

I followed Arthur down the street trying not to touch him but keeping a little back from him, but he soon took hold of my arm and started talking about the film we were going to see. I hardly heard a word he said, I had thoughts of rape . . . dope . . . white slave traffic even ... all the lurid stories from the women's magazines rose up before me. Before I knew it we were on a bus and he was buying two tickets to LONDON ! I sat as near to the window as I could leaving a gap between us and I stubbornly looked out of the window hardly bothering to speak to him. We alighted at Trafalgar Square and I had to admit that I felt more excited than frightened as we walked towards a large cinema in Leicester Square.

There were crowds outside and photographers with flashing lights taking photos of various people entering the cinema. The posters announced that tonight was a FILM PREMIERE and I realised that the photographers were there because some of the film stars were ... I found that I was now clinging tightly to Arthur who just smiled down at me and calmly walked into the foyer of the glistening palace. I know the film starred Bing Crosby but what it was about I had no idea. My mind was in a turmoil - what a tale to tell Marjorie tomorrow. But there was more to come. After the show we had a meal in a restaurant in Charing Cross Road. Once again I was so overcome with my surroundings that I had no idea what I ate. This was my very first meal in a restaurant, I had never seen so much cutlery for two people before. Arthur asked me what I wanted to drink and as the only beverage I had ever seen drunk with a cooked meal was when Dad had a beer, I asked for a light ale. The waiter flinched visibly but Arthur calmly ordered it and one for himself as well. The rest of the evening went in a flash and Arthur was walking me back up the street, over the cobbles, and I was being kissed, this time very expertly for the first time in my life - and

I liked it. But our lovemaking went no further than kissing and a few moments later I was dazedly stumbling upstairs to my bedroom to re-live the night over and over again.

So begun my education into the good things of life with Arthur. He advised me on the right shade of lipstick to wear with what dress . . . we went dancing, to the theatre, we had dinner with friends of his (fancy calling it dinner at eight o'clock at night!) and we went dog-racing and one memorable day was spent on Epsom Downs for Derby Day. For Arthur was, I soon found out, a many sided individual and he loved gambling as much as he did good food and well dressed women. His own outward appearance was the result of many years training by his widowed mother. A very hard working woman, who had built a career up for herself in a London firm, and had brought her only son up to be the well spoken, well dressed idol that he now presented to the world. I realised when I met her that among her desires for the best of everything for her boy was of course The Right Girl ... and I was certainly not classified as that. For one thing I came from the wrong end of town and lived in a street far beneath the status of theirs. Their houses were not much bigger than ours but they all had a tiny patch of front garden and many of them had bathrooms. Arthur turned out to be not only a success with Mum but my brother Fred found him a worthy companion also as he too was a gambler. Soon they met regularly at Charlton or Catford for the Friday night greyhound races, and even Dad was not left out of things for long. Arthur made only one mistake with Dad ... he arrived one night bearing a bottle of beer for him. This was an error of enormous proportions to Dad ... bottled beer was on a level with ready-made cigarettes in his book. However a quick drinking session down at the Crown soon put Arthur straight with Dad. So after all I was a dutiful daughter - I had found Mr Right. Well that is what the family and friends thought but somehow I knew that Arthur would never be my complete world.

When he received his calling up papers I did realise how much I would miss him but he never suggested us getting engaged, in fact we did not discuss marrying, or our future life together at all at anytime. We kept up a regular correspondence throughout the first few months and when he came home on leave he looked so handsome in his naval uniform that I felt really proud to be seen out with him. On our last night at the Greenwich Town Hall dance I wore a new red frock, and I knew how envious my girl friends were of my good looking sailor. During the afternoon I had shown off some of the presents he had given to me ... a leather handbag, real silk stockings, perfume ... After the dance during the walk home he said that he wished I had used one of his gifts that evening. Which one I asked ... apparently in the handbag was a small leather wallet that contained about a dozen different lipsticks, their colours ranging from pale orange, through the pinks to ruby red and deep burgundy ... it would have made it easier, he said, to have got the exact shade to match my dress - the one I was wearing clashed too much.

131

CHAPTER THIRTY SEVEN

It came as a shock to walk into the office one Monday morning to find a complete stranger sitting at my desk. A very sophisticated mature woman, beautifully dressed with a marvellous complexion. I learned after a few days close scrutiny this was due to using much less powder and rouge than I had thought one needed.

But on that first morning I stood and stared, rudely demanding what she was doing at my desk. Dear Mrs Haddon came across to me and pointed out another desk facing my old one.

"Don't you remember Mr Lakey saying we were having extra help with the progress chasing, this is Mrs Markham".

It did not take long to see that I was now the Junior progress chaser. Mrs Markham was an experienced, well-educated woman and if I had not been so full of my own self importance I would have known that this factory with its tremendous increase of war work could not rely upon a seventeen year old girl to run this ever expanding side of the buying office.

But still being young my pride came first and I became full of bitter resentment, mostly against the one who had least to blame, Mrs Markham. I sat and watched her make the very important telephone calls to chase urgent supplies whilst I waded through the paper part of the job. I was back to filing again, the only saving grace being that they were very important files that I now handled.

One afternoon Mr Lakey returned from a farewell lunch with one of the captains of the cable ships and within a few moments of reaching his office he demanded one of my files. I took it in to him and was about to leave the office when I felt a thump on my shoulder, it was the file which had been thrown in disgust at me. With papers flying down on to the carpet I was yelled at, "Bloody fool, blast your eyes, can't you get me a simple thing like a file when I want it". It was the expression "blast your eyes" that sent my temper rising, I hated it when he shouted it at one or other of us and it was one of his most frequent curses. I heard myself scream back, "Get your own bloody file and keep your bloody old job - I hate you."

Back once again in the outer office Mrs Haddon tried to console me but it was no use. I grabbed my bag and coat and ran, ran all the way along the yard, past the gang of men who were pushing a huge cable drum out of the works, ran on and on up Christchurch Street across the main road and straight on up my own cobbled street until I reached home. Of course Mum was there and wanted to know what had happened but I was too full of tears to tell her. She took me upstairs and I lay down waiting for the sobs to stop long enough to tell her what had happened. She was marvellous, never told me off at all, just said that when I went back in the morning it would probably all be forgotten. And she went downstairs to make a cup of tea.

The next morning I sat silently at my desk, sorting out papers without ever seeing them. Within a few minutes the buzzer sounded four times, my signal. I was shaking as I entered his office but he just sat there with a queer smile on his face.

"So, you no longer want to work here?"

He had not been too drunk to remember what I had said then, immediately I felt the resentment rising inside me. If he hadn't been so drunk why had he behaved so badly. But I only remarked that I was not so happy since Mrs Markham had taken over the job. He told me he had no intention of letting her go. I said nothing. He wondered if I would like a transfer to another office. At that my ego sank ... he was prepared to let me go and keep her ...

"I think it better if I leave altogether - there are plenty of jobs going, and", I added, " I have learnt a lot whilst working here."

" If you really want to, then I certainly won't stop you, and you're right, you have learnt a lot and very well too. I know you will get on well whatever you do next, just tell your new boss to telephone me for a reference. I think you are ready for more than I can offer you, but not quite ready to take over a top position like Mrs Markham."

He gave me a beautiful soft grey leather wallet as a goodbye present and I used it for many years always remembering him and how much he taught me.

Of course when I broke the news after tea to Mum and Dad all hell broke loose but I shut myself up in my bedroom and played my latest King Oliver record over and over again until Dad forgot the original row and threatened to come upstairs and put his fist through the gramophone if I didn't stop that bloody row!

The following Monday morning, dressed in my best, I waited for a tram to take me to the Labour Exchange. Coming towards me was old Whistling Joe pushing his rusty bike which had only one flat tyre which was on the front wheel, the rear one ran on its rims very bent and buckled. Incredible as it seems there were days when you could actually see Joe riding this contraption and as he bumped and rattled past the kids would shout and whistle after him.

He was a rag and bone man, one of the many that walked the streets daily pushing bikes or barrows. He had got his name from Old Bill, our Gran's lodger, who also roamed the streets and riverside. During school holidays I often accompanied Old Bill and we would pick up all pins, because they were lucky as well as useful, and we collected a vast assortment of buttons and a few foreign coins. We often found farthings and halfpennies and of course we collected fag-ends. These Bill carefully emptied every evening into an old Oxo tin. He boasted that he never bought tobacco, only fag-papers.

Through Bill I got to know the rag and bone men and in later years I often embarrassed my friends when walking through the town we would suddenly hear a hoarse chuckle followed by "Allo me old mate, ows fings then". Whistling Joe was even more embarrassing as you could only hear him properly if he put his face close up to yours. His voice was now only a whisper followed by a whistling sound that emerged from the depths of his hollow chest.

I was in no mood for one of his chats this morning and hoped that a tram would arrive in time to save our meeting. But as he plodded on and on towards the tram stop I saw the other two women standing there shake their heads in pity at him. Then he recognised me and with a shaky grin, his stubbly old chin trembling he eagerly thrust his face close to mine - and immediately the two women stepped back in horror.

"Wot yer doing - skylarking from work gal", he wheezed. "I fort you worked down there", he pointed towards the cable factory at the bottom of Christchurch Street.

"Not any more Joe", I said, "here comes a tram, must catch it, I am after another job."

I thankfully stepped off the pavement but he held my arm grinning, "Why not come and help me like you used to?" and he went off into gasps of whistling laughter.

I shook my head and jumped on to the tram following the other women who obviously wanted to get as far away from me as well as Joe. But he had not given up, he came alongside the tram and rested his bike against it, stopping the conductor from ringing the bell for us to start.

The old man leaned over the steps of the tram and said to me and the rest of the passengers, "Ole Robbo wants someone to do all that typing stuff, go and see 'im", he muttered on mostly to himself, "they tell me his secketery went after a row wiv him".

By this time the conductor had lost his patience and he jumped off the tram, took the bike away and laid it on the pavement. Then shaking his fist at Joe he returned to the tram, rang the bell heartily and we were off. No-one was more thankful than I when with a burning face I left the tram at Deptford Bridge.

I was made to feel uncomfortable again when interviewed regarding another job. The clerk made it clear that I was obviously mad in giving up a good job and he also made it by stating categorically that there was no office work available at all and I was to come back next week.

Walking back home I wondered how Dad would react when he heard my news. Up to now he had been surprisingly calm about the whole affair ... in fact I had played into his hands somewhat. He said that Mr Lakey's treatment of me would show how those office wallahs stuck together and it was always the outsider that took the can back. I knew he would not allow me to be without work for long and I would soon find myself back in Siemens or another factory like it if another job did not materialise soon. When I reached St Alphege's church I decided to cut through Greenwich Market and walk home by the riverside. I suddenly remembered Whistling Joe's last remark about Ole Robbo needing a secretary and it made me smile, because I had played as a kid all around Robinson's Scrap Yard and never even seen an office. Everyone in Greenwich knew the yard, it contained enormous stacks of rusty metal which seemed to have taken root. They had always looked the same as long as I could remember, never getting smaller or larger. And yet every day one old man after another would push their barrows into the yard with more and more bits of rusty pieces to sell to Robbo.

The scrap yard was just a few yards in front of me along the towpath and instead of walking by I found myself wandering among the piles of scrap. Suddenly shouting emerged from a small tin hut which was situated on the muddy bit of shore just out of reach of the incoming tide. The door of the hut flew open and out ran a young boy, closely followed by a large book which flew through the air just missing the back of his head. A man appeared in the doorway shouting and shaking his head, he saw me and yelled, "What the hell do you want?"

My first reaction was to follow the little boy but so desperate was my need for a job I found myself asking if he required a secretary. He invited me inside. Once at his desk he became a different person, apologised for his behaviour with the office boy who 'was enough to try the patience of a saint' and the interview went very smoothly. He went over to a second desk which was covered with piles of paper and replaced the telephone directory that he had thrown at the boy, then to my surprise he seemed to disappear through the wall. I noticed then that the walls and woodwork were so dark and dirty that a door leading off to another office was almost invisible. After a short while he came back and told me to go into this outer office. There sitting in a big armchair was a very old man. He was in his shirt sleeves which were rolled up. There was no desk, but in one corner stood a table with a typewriter on it. The room was very dismal and untidy and I began to have doubts about the sanity of the old man as he just sat looking down at the floor. After a few minutes he raised his head and in really foul language called out for someone. I could hardly hear because another row had started up in the next office. The man who had interviewed me came back into the room and told the old man to shut up; in reply the old man told him to get out of his sight. And then turning to me he started to tell me that his secretary had left him after almost twenty years ... I realised then that the old man was the one who wanted the secretary. I got the job but I had to take quite a cut in salary.

When I told Mum I was Robbo's secretary she looked so pleased and even when I explained the lower salary she said, "Never mind, everyone knows they never pay much."

Well if I didn't get much money I also did not have to work very hard. The first morning I arrived to find there were in fact two men working in the main office, but they seemed to spend a lot of time shouting at each other and cursing the office boy. As the day wore on the swearing and throwing of objects seemed to be the only signs of life in the hut. And this continued for three days. I just sat at my table and the old man sat in his chair. I asked if he wanted me to do anything, but I never got an answer. I started to do some tidying up and offered to help the men in the other office but they wanted nothing to do with me and told me stay with the old man. On the afternoon of the third day the old man dictated a letter to Boosey and Hawkes for some violin strings. I asked if he was the musician and he just nodded. The next day he had the violin on his lap and now and again played a few notes on it. During the afternoon the sirens sounded for an air raid. There was no shelter but I was told that I could go to the nearest one in the next street if I wanted to. I decided to stay where I was and not go running out into the open. Through the dusty window that day I saw my very first German aeroplane, it was yellow with a black cross on it, the old man said it was a Meschersmitt. It flew low over the river and was machine-gunning as it went ... later on we heard that it had crashed near a school between West Greenwich and Deptford.

Naturally this incident was a great talking point around our tea table that night. Dad said he had seen the plane as it followed the course of the river and I said I had seen it too. Together Mum and Dad said this was impossible. I told them I had been close enough to see the yellow and black markings. Dad looked puzzled, "Where were you then?"

"In my office."

"Rubbish, don't I keep on telling you it bleedin' well crashed before it got to Deptford."

There was a long silence, then Mum said "You told me you were working at Robinson's. "I am."

"Well, if their flour mills ain't at Deptford, where are they?"

"Not Robinson's Flour Mills, Old Robbo's, you know, the junkyard." I sat back and looked at both of their bewildered faces - there was an ominous silence which ended with Dad suddenly crashing his fist down among the tea things and shouting at me. Why did I deliberately go and show the family up in this way? How many times did I think he would put up with my coming and going with this job and that? Mum could not really believe that her daughter was secretary to a junk man instead of a millowner. She wondered what Daisy would say when she heard about it. I cared very little what Daisy thought about me or my job. Most of my friends thought I was lucky to be getting paid for doing nothing. But I was bored. For the next two weeks I sat at my table and the old man sat in his chair, now and again playing a few notes on his violin. I decided to ask for Friday afternoon off and go to the Labour Exchange to see if there were any more jobs available.

But they beat me to it. On Thursday night Mum handed me a letter from them. It was a small printed leaflet informing me to attend an interview with them on the following Monday morning.

I duly presented myself with the letter and was shown into a room containing a few wooden chairs, a table around which sat two men and one woman, all middle aged, and there was a chair opposite them into which I was directed.

I was questioned about my various jobs, why I had left them, what work could I do, had I passed any examinations. One man never spoke, just looked through a file. The questions stopped and this man looked up. "Well," he said, "you don't seem to be able to settle down, do you?" Before I could answer the woman whispered something to him and he went on. "I am afraid your present occupation is not essential war work and you must leave it."

I nodded cheerfully and was about to speak but the woman started before me, "You are a lucky girl really. We can give you a choice of three ... there is plenty of work in a munitions factory in Darlington ... or you could train as a nurse, they are extremely short in mental nursing ... or failing either of those you will be conscripted into the A.T.S. Let us know by Wednesday morning, be here at 9. 30am."

I stood outside on the pavement not realising that I had left the room and walked downstairs. Called up for the Army, me, impossible. But it wasn't. A week later I found myself having my first army medical in a house in Chelsea. All the gruesome tales gleefully told by Dad were, I found, only tales. Before going to the medical I made a couple of abortive attempts to join the W.A.A.F. and the W.R.N.S., when I realised that so strong was my aversion to going into a factory that I would indeed rather go into the services. The idea became quite exciting for here after all was the chance to get right away from my surroundings, the one thing I had wanted for so long. The W.A.A. F. recruiting officer sadly informed me that they were not taking any more girls for sometime as they had enough. The W.R.N.S. were shorter and sharper in their reply when they realised how little education I had had and also to my discredit was the fact that I had no relative serving in the Royal Navy.

Dad gave me a farewell session in the Crown and even Molly the pub cook came into the bar to say goodbye.

Marjorie and some of the dancing crowd took me out during the interval of my last Town Hall Dance and all too soon it was Monday morning and I was standing alone on Maze Hill Station waiting for the train to Charing Cross. I was on my way to my first camp at Guildford. It had been decided that it was not worth either Mum or Dad losing wages by taking time off to see me go and our goodbyes had been said earlier in the morning. As I boarded the train the last thing I saw was the four pinnacled tower of Christ Church - the last landmark for a farewell wave to my street.